C000186117

POLITICS AND PARANOIA

By ROBIN RAMSAY

First published in Great Britain 2008 by Picnic Publishing
PO Box 5222, Hove BN52 9LP

A catalogue record for this book is available from the British Library.

ISBN: 9780955610547

Printed and bound in Great Britain by RPM Print & Design

CONTENTS

INTRODUCTION

Since 1983 I have edited and published the magazine *Lobster*, which began trying to cover what used to be called parapolitics: secret intelligence organisations and their influence on history, covert operations, 'hidden' history, official secrets – that sort of thing – and has changed slowly over the years to include politics and even sprinklings of economics, as well as British and international politics. While producing *Lobster* has been my core activity, I have written books on conspiracy theories, the assassination of JFK, three books on the recent history of the Labour Party, written for other publications, and I have given occasional talks. Because I am unable to do a talk just from notes – I tried it once, with disastrous results – I have always written the talks out. This book is a collection of those talks, the earliest from 1986.

I got into these fields by accident. In 1976 or 7 the now defunct 'underground' magazine, *International Times*, ran, as a comic strip, a now infamous American conspiracy theory called The Skeleton Key to the Gemstone File. It was the first conspiracy theory I had come across and was very striking. But unlike the rest of my little group of dope-smoking chums in Hull who merely said, 'Wow, man. Far out', I went into the University of Hull library to see if it was true. (I had been a student there from 1971-74.) Of course, as with most conspiracy theories, much of Gemstone was uncheckable and what was checkable proved to be mostly nonsense. (I wrote a critique of Gemstone which *International Times* ran in one of their final issues.) But while rummaging around in the American history section of the library, I came across all manner of strange and interesting material of which I had previously been unaware; and when I became unemployed shortly thereafter, I began a serious self-education programme, beginning with post-war American history. Following the never-ending trail of footnote references, I wandered into the cold war, nuclear strategic theory, intelligence agencies and so forth. I spent the best part of 6 years signing-on the dole and reading books and journals.

Among the treasures in the University of Hull library was a pristine set of the 26 volumes of evidence and exhibits from the Warren Commission's investigation into the assassination of JFK. I began taking them out, two or three at a time, and eventually read/skimmed my way through the entire set. I learned little from them – without a guide through them they are an incomprehensible mess – but an interest in the Kennedy assassination was born. There is one talk in this collection on that event and it looms large in several of the others.

My interest in the Kennedy assassination led me to the tiny British network of JFK buffs, notably the late Harry Irwin, who produced a newsletter on the subject and shovelled books out to the network members. (Harry was a book scout/dealer.) Harry connected to me to Steve Dorril, another JFK buff, who was living in Huddersfield. We met and decided to produce our own newsletter. Steve chose the name *Lobster*. Since I was unemployed and had the time, and Steve had a job and thus a bit of money, we agreed that I would produce it and he would subsidise it if necessary. Thus from issue one I did all the work and the editing; and, in the event, it never needed subsidising by Steve.

Lobster began as an A5 pamphlet. The text was typed, reduced on a photocopier and then printed off-set. (For younger readers, this is in the days before PCs and computer printers; getting a text typeset was very expensive.) The first few issues were printed by a friend of mine in Hull, Colin Challen, now an MP. Slowly *Lobster* grew in size and circulation and got into a few bookshops. Other people began writing for it. At issue 9 it went from A5 up to A4. Things got more expensive and I had to appeal for money from *Lobster*'s little group of subscribers. One of them, the novelist and playwright G. F. Newman, sent me £80 – which seemed like a lot of money at the time and which bailed us out. I never needed to appeal again.

In the period covered by issues 9, 10 and 11, 1985/86, two significant things happened. Steve made contact with former British Army Captain Fred Holroyd, and, through Fred, with Colin Wallace, a former psy-ops officer in the British Army, then in Lewes prison for a manslaughter he didn't commit. Fred and Colin began educating us about events in Northern Ireland – and about events in the UK in the mid 1970s, the events which became known as 'the Wilson plots': the machinations by a loose alliance of the Tory Right, British capital, sections of the British, American and South African intelligence services and the British military, against the Labour government led by Harold Wilson. This tiny magazine in Hull, produced by me while living on the dole, with absolutely no resources, had stumbled across an enormous story. The second significant event was Steve agreeing to write a book about the Profumo Affair with well known non-fiction author, Anthony Summers. (The Profumo Affair, the scandal in which the Tory Minister for War, John Profumo, was discovered to be sharing a young woman, Christine Keeler, with a Soviet intelligence officer, was one of Steve's interests and he had written a piece about it in *Lobster 2*.) As a result of beginning work on the book, Steve's contribution to *Lobster* began to diminish. The relationship with Holroyd and Wallace begun by Steve devolved to me and I wrote *Lobster* 11 about 'the Wilson plots'.

In the space of six months Steve had become a full-time book writer with his share of the publisher's advance for what became the Dorril-Summers book *Honeytrap*, and I began what became four years of virtually full-time work trying to understand, amplify and explain to others the significance of what Colin Wallace had to tell us about the British state's activities in Northern Ireland and the role they played in the anti-Labour operations of the mid 1970s. Steve and I wrote the book *Smear! Wilson and the Secret State* (London 1991) about those anti-Labour operations. After which Steve began writing another book and I continued producing the magazine. Eventually, when Steve's contributions to the magazine had all but ceased, I took his name off it and stopped pretending that *Lobster* was two of us.

The subject matter of the talks in this volume echoes some of the central themes I have written about and published; American parapolitics; claims of mind control technology; the rise to prominence of conspiracy theories in our culture; the influence of the British and American secret states on British politics; and the collapse of the Labour Party into its present neo-conservative vacuity. The last two themes are linked quite directly: it was always the aim of the British secret state, British capital and the American state to remove all radical impulses from the Labour Party if they could.

Looked at another way, these essays show someone who became interested in British politics and history after being interested first in the history and politics of post-WW2 America; not the textbook history, but history as seen by a small group of researchers for whom the 'real' history of those years was partly or completely hidden or suppressed. Of this group the biggest single influence was Professor Peter Dale Scott, a former Canadian diplomat who became first an American English academic and poet and later, during the Vietnam War, began researching the origins of that war. This led him into parapolitics, the term he coined to describe these subject areas.

This collection's title is apposite: one of my first attempts in these fields was a pamphlet in 1981 titled 'In defence of paranoia (again)', acknowledging Carl Oglesby's seminal essay in the American independent left magazine *Ramparts* in 1973, 'In defence of paranoia', to which I refer a number of times in these talks. In a sense I have spent the last 25 years reworking themes I first came across in Oglesby.

Although in a few places I have removed names to avoid potential libels, I have not tried to edit these essays. This means the reader can see my errors – some of which I comment on – and the repetition of ideas (and, occasionally, paragraphs as material was cannibalised).

Thanking people for their help is always risky because any list will be incomplete; but the curious intellectual journey I have undertaken would have been much more difficult without travelling companions Anthony Frewin and John Booth; and impossible without the support of Sally Walker.

Robin Ramsay
May 2008

CHAPTER ONE

In Defence of Paranoia: Rationality and Mind Control

Paranoia Network Conference, Manchester Metropolitan University, 2004.

In 1973 Carl Oglesby had an essay published in the American magazine *Ramparts*. At that time *Ramparts* was the leading American left-radical magazine and Oglesby was well known – in some circles – for his previous role in SDS, Students for a Democratic Society. Oglesby's essay appeared towards the beginning of what became known as Watergate and his thesis was that the American Left, then preoccupied with the war in Vietnam, should be paying more attention to domestic events such as Watergate and the assassinations in the 1960s of John Kennedy, Robert Kennedy and Martin Luther King, none of which, Oglesby correctly argued, had been adequately investigated. His essay's title, 'In Defence of Paranoia', the title I chose for this talk when asked for one, was a reference to, and an implied rejection of, a famous essay of a decade before by the historian Richard Hofstadter, 'The Paranoid Style in American Politics'. While specifically aimed at the radical *Right* of the time, especially the John Birch Society, Hofstadter's essay linked an interest in conspiracies or conspiracy theories with paranoia and with the loony radical Right. Hofstader thus helped to *contaminate* the subjects for the liberal-Left which then – and now – is unwilling to be associated with almost anything on or of the Right.

Hofstader's influential and widely discussed essay reinforced existing academic and intellectual prejudices which allotted to an interest in conspiracy theories or actual conspiracies the intellectual status of – say – spiritualism: of interest only to the stupid, the uneducated or the ill. For 'serious' people – academics, journalists, politicians – large areas of political inquiry have been contaminated ever since by an association with conspiracy theories. Hofstader's essay appeared just when questions were being asked about the assassination of JFK and his essay helped to shore up the 'lone assassin' verdict offered by the Warren Commission.

Carl Oglesby's 'In Defence of Paranoia' was written during the Watergate scandal which triggered a long series of Congressional inquiries. The most important of these were those into the CIA which revealed mind control projects, plans to assassinate foreign leaders, subvert or manipulate the world's trade unions, left movements and the world's media; and a parallel inquiry which revealed the FBI's Cointelpro programme of infiltration and disruption of the radical Left (and Right), though mostly the Left. There was also an incompetent congressional inquiry into the assassination of JFK and Martin Luther King.

By 1978, it had been established – by *Congress* – that during the Cold War America had behaved in a similar way to its Cold War enemy, the Soviet Union. By 1978, it had been established – by *Congress* – that the real political world had turned out to be pretty much the way some of 'the paranoids' thought it was.

The consensus reality of politics, the reporting and agenda of politics, and the academic study of politics, should have changed: but they didn't, not really. Not a single academic American historian has looked at the assassinations of the 1960s. The handful of American academics who have, are not historians.

Despite the fact that the revelations of the 1970s had shown that, to quote the late Abbie Hoffman, conspiracy was as American as apple pie, the accusation of 'conspiracy theorising' remained a powerful term of abuse. Robert Parry, then working for *Newsweek* magazine, discovered this in 1985 when he began digging into what became known as Iran-Contra, the secret White House programme of selling weapons to Iran to raise money for the war against Nicaragua. *Newsweek*'s managing editor, and Parry's boss, was wined and dined by the White House, where he was told that Parry was just a wacky conspiracy theorist, signalling the end of Parry's *Newsweek* job.

I began taking an interest in these areas in 1976, since when I have been been working with material much of whose content has been regarded as paranoid by the guardians of our political consensus, the political reality gatekeepers. In the fields I am interested in, there is the added difficulty that most of the major players are committed to secrecy (while talking of openness); and the intelligence services are committed to secrecy and disinforming us about their activities.

In 1981, in explicit homage to Oglesby, but addressing an imaginary British rather than American left audience, I published a pamphlet called *In Defence of Paranoia (again)*. Two years after that I began publishing a magazine called *Lobster* which tried to look at the activities of covert groups, intelligence agencies, secret societies and agendas - what became known around then as parapolitics. The climax of this phase of my activities was the work in 1986-90 on what became known as the Wilson plots – a misleading but inevitable title for a collection of interrelated subjects in the parapolitics of Britain in the 1970s.

At its root was the belief on the Tory Right and its allies among the intelligence and security services, that Britain, under Prime Minister Harold Wilson, was on the verge of a Soviet take-over; and this justified any kind of political action. In the clubs of London they believed that the survival of Britain – really they meant England; and really really they meant London and the Home Counties – was under threat. This anti-Communist conspiracy theory of British politics went like this: the Soviets control the British Communist Party; the British CP controls the trade unions; and the trade unions control the Labour Party. Thus the Soviets control the Labour Party. The result of this conspiracy theory, this paranoia on the right, was the events of 1973-9, widespread bugging and burglaries of Labour cabinet members and trade unionists; disinformation and smear campaigns; the formation of so-called private armies and rumours of coups. It was a major rattling of sabres on the right, which climaxed in the election of a true believer in the theory, Mrs Thatcher. It was the British Watergate – or could have been had it been pursued more seriously by the major media and the Labour Party when it was pointed out to them by people like me.

Towards the end of this period, in 1989, I received a phone call from an American called Harlan Girard. He was in London and had been advised to ring me. He had been going round the London media trying to interest it in the subject of mind control. He got nowhere, of course, was given the bum's rush and passed on to someone else. Eventually someone suggested me and my magazine, circulation about 1000, right at the bottom of the media pile. Would I talk to him? Sure, I said. Come to see me in Hull. This was my standard response: if you can be bothered to travel to me, I will talk to you. Most people, of course, can't be bothered. Which is the point. But Harlan turned up lugging two suitcases full of photocopied documents and told me a very strange story about being harassed by the CIA using microwaves. He was getting voices: people were talking to him, mocking him, directing him.

For the consensus reality of sanity and madness, Harlan Girard was mad, a schizophrenic – voices, for Christ's sake! But though I had never heard of microwave voices, I had three books on my shelves which had given me enough to put the madness diagnosis on hold. There was the 1979 John Marks book, *The Search for the Manchurian Candidate*, which described the

CIA's MK Ultra programmes in the 1950s and 60s. Alarmed by the phenomenon of 'brain washing' during the Korean War by the Chinese, the CIA had begun seriously researching the brain and how to manipulate and defend it against manipulation. The agency began looking at drugs, hypnosis, stress – the whole spectrum. Although the files were destroyed during the Watergate affair, traces of the programme survived in duplicate files in the CIA and a heavily edited version of the existing fragments was released by the CIA in 1977. There was also Walter Bowart's *Operation Mind Control*, much more speculative, which included a very striking account of US Navy research into zombie assassins; and there was *The Control of Candy Jones* which purported to be the true story of a woman who had been programmed by the CIA, using drugs and hypnosis, and worked as a courier for the Agency. If captured she didn't know her real name, let alone anything about what she was carrying or for whom. The CIA – if the story was true – had created an 'alter', a multiple personality.

So when Harlan Girard told me this weird story about the CIA talking to him through microwaves, I knew just enough to know that this wasn't *totally* off the wall. About microwaves I knew nothing. But I knew that the Soviet and NATO military and intelligence agencies had been trying to find ways to control and manipulate the human brain.

Harlan stayed the night and left me a collection of photocopies which showed that whatever the status of his personal story – whether fantasy, hallucination or not

– what he was describing, that is the projection of voices into a human brain, inaudible to anyone else, was physically possible. The basic research had been done in 1960/61. And thus Harlan's story might be true. And this is what I very carefully announced in the next issue of my magazine. That was 15 years ago. Since when I have accumulated a lot more documents in this field and have met and corresponded with more people claiming to be microwave victims.

Let me digress slightly here. Before the microwave stage, the US military was trying to develop very small receiver-transmitters which could be implanted in the human skull. In 1970 NASA, which was developing them for possible use in space travel, had got these things down to the size of a one penny piece. One was implanted in a Swede called Robert Naeslund, who has spent over 20 years trying to persuade the Swedes to take his story seriously, without success. You can see the implants and pictures and X-rays of the surgery to have it removed, on the net. Although a number of people have claimed to have been implanted, I am not aware of any other clear-cut example. Implants seem to have been abandoned, overtaken by the microwave technology in the mid-1980s. My understanding is that implants could never work anyway.

It isn't clear how widespread was the early microwave work: no government agency has discussed what it was doing, no-one from the programmes has admitted working on it. The most prominent agency in the early scientific research was the US Navy, which was interested in low frequency waves as a possible means of communicating with their submarines.[1]

There is now a large body of work, much of it on the Net, on the scientific basis of this phenomenon. On a larger scale its military use is no longer a secret. The US military has a squadron of planes, called Commando Solo, kitted-out with the equipment made by the Silent Sound corporation, which is used to broadcast psychological warfare messages, psy-ops, on microwave beams. It was used during the first Gulf War in 1991, and is alleged to have been used since in conflicts in Haiti and Yugoslavia. I don't know whether it works or not; there appears to be no publicly available evaluation of it. Incidentally, Silent Sound Inc. used to have a website on which they advertised this technology. While writing this I looked it up: it appears to have been taken down. However the patent on which the technology is based is still on the Net and there are many references to the equipment and the squadron.

What is denied – what is simply not officially *discussed* – is that this technology, operational in 1991, has been used on individuals. Yet it must have been tried out on people while being developed. So this is my guess: *some* of those claiming to have suffered microwave mind control, who claim to be getting voices in their heads, have simply been unwitting subjects in military experiments. But only some. I have met people and read accounts by people I did not believe. But how do I distinguish between them and the people I do believe? Before writing this talk I hadn't considered this; I had just done it.

I have known one acute schizophrenic, a woman I had known for 20 years when she became ill. She began ringing me up and delivering high speed babble, intensely complex and totally unintelligible stories about a vast masonic conspiracy to destroy her life. These monologues were remarkable things: I couldn't talk that fast with a script and a week's rehearsal. She just turned on some kind of tap and out it poured. She was the first – and so far the only – schizophrenic I have known well. She was given drugs and the drugs began to turn the babble off. The earlier person re-emerged, not quite the same person, of course; and a very shaky person, not least because of the side-effects of these drugs; but the earlier person.

My point is not merely to irritate those present for whom 'schizophrenic' is a problematic term; my point is that she was schizophrenic all the way through. Totally consistent. It affected every aspect of her all the time. She didn't just have a bad ten minutes. Some of the people I have met claiming to be hearing microwave voices, are quite ordinary, 'sane', in the other aspects of their life and conversations. Their 'odd ideas' only extend to this. When I think of the various people I have met making these claims it is those I have taken seriously. I am still where I was in 1989: given that the technology exists to do this, it might be happening.

Let me give you a brief sketch of a couple of them. There is Harlan, the American, just turned sixty, who trained originally as a landscape architect. There is a Chinese-Scotsman, with a degree in biology, now running a Chinese takeaway in Aberdeen. He drove about 300 miles to see me, Aberdeen to Hull, after the briefest of phone conversations. When I opened the door his first words were: 'Can you turn it off?' Of course I couldn't. He rummaged through my files, made some copies, and drove home again. He reported that flying East out of the UK, the signal, the beam he was getting, only stopped when he reached Turkish airspace.

There is a computer software developer, a serious Christian. He tells me that when he was in South Africa recently the signal, the beam, stopped and restarted just when his mobile phone told him it was going in and out of range of *its* signal. This may be a significant discovery: perhaps the signal is being piggybacked on the mobile phone networks. These reports of microwave mind control rise in parallel with the spread of mobile phone networks.

I met these three, with a fourth I didn't know, and spent an afternoon talking about this. At one point I asked them how many were being beamed at while we talked: two put their hands up. I have had conversations with Harlan Girard in which there were three parties apparently present: me, him and what he calls his handlers, who commented, through him, on our conversation. How this was done – assuming it *was* done – remains a mystery. The people who find themselves getting these voices are obsessed by two questions: Why me? And how are they doing it? The Chinese Scot I referred to earlier concluded at one point that it had been done by satellites: there could be no other way of keeping him in a beam all the time. Other victims don't believe this.

Harlan has been in contact with over a hundred people claiming to be experiencing this, mostly in the US. I asked him if there was any distinguishing features to this group. There was only one he could see: none of them seemed to be gay. (Though how would he know?)

These tales of implants in the body and microwaved mind-control have other reverberations. There are other stories of implants, allegedly the work of extraterrestrials, aliens, which began to appear in American UFOlogy in the late 1980s. One clever American, Martin Cannon, noticing that several of the accounts of being implanted sounded more like a terrestrial military operation than anything to do with extraterrestrials, wondered if the alien story was simply set-dressing, a cover-story for the US military's implant trials.

The invisible beam from a microwave whispering instructions and abuse inside your head, Harlan Girard's three-way conversations with me and his handlers, has an obvious analogy with the psychic and the spirit guide: another invisible third party apparently communicating. There are also analogies here with the claims of alien abduction – more invisible third parties. Like some of the mind control victims, many of those claiming to have been abducted by aliens are apparently pretty ordinary – 'sane' people most of the time.

I offer these speculations merely because they are striking, not because I have any idea what it all means. Thousands of people, mostly Americans, claimed to have been abducted by aliens in the last 20 years. Most of them found the experience terrifying; most of them did not want to be identified. Some of them claimed to have been implanted during their experience. Yet as far as I am aware no indisputably alien implant has been recovered; and no alien abduction has been seen taking place, let alone recorded on videotape. The only 'abduction' I have read of which *was* witnessed, consisted of the 'abductee' falling asleep and, on waking, claiming to have been abducted.

There is a profound mystery here, a fact recognised by a couple of brave American academics, Jacobs and Mack, who tried to investigate the subject and received a torrent of abuse and ridicule from their colleagues and the media for doing so.

All these people – mind-control victims, alleged abductees, implant victims – would be dismissed as paranoid – at best – by most people and most mental health professionals; just as in the 1960s most of those who pored over the photographs taken on Dealey Plaza and combed through the Warren Commission's 26 volumes of evidence, and thought there was a conspiracy in Dallas to murder JFK, were dismissed as paranoid.

About most of the nature of reality there is general agreement. The kettle boils only when it is switched on. But bits of it are contested. What is going on? What is the political world like? What does history consist of? What really happened? In this contest over the nature of reality, paranoia is a terribly useful term to our consensus reality gatekeepers. In politics it is used to marginalise and denigrate anything which suggests that our political masters and our political system is anything other than a series of well-intentioned individuals and happenstance. Cock-up or conspiracy is the choice, we are told; and the self-selected sophisticates of our world always choose cock-up. Men – and women – of the world, the concept implies, know that people mess everything up; conspiracies don't exist. Human affairs are a muddle, too complex to be amenable to the machinations of small groups of people.

Despite the assassinations of the 1960s, Watergate, the CIA revelations, Cointelpro, Koreagate, Iran-Contra, the Wilson plots, the now acknowledged conspiracy between the British Army and the Ulster protestants in the 1980s to murder Catholics; the now acknowledged action of the CIA and the US Attorney General in allowing the importation of cocaine into America by dealers who gave money to the war against Nicaragua; after all this – and the list could be expanded almost infinitely – after all these examples of actual political conspiracies, it remains one of the bedrock beliefs of our chattering classes that people interested in political conspiracies are paranoid. 'Conspiracy theorist' retains its potency as a put-down.

Discussing the possible publication of a book on 9-11, an editor in a London publisher e-mailed me recently:

'There is further an enormous reluctance among publishers to stick their necks out in areas like this. After all, if true, the 9-11 conspiracy renders the last 3 years of history into a nightmarish farce. Consciously or not, publishers exist inside the dominant narratives of their

culture. Even if someone was to write a sober and careful examination of the evidence that drew on highly author-itative sources, there are very few mainstream editors in London (perhaps none in the corporations, funnily enough) who would touch it. Editors tend to be very sensitive to accusations of being "conspiracy theorists". . . Publish a book about Diana, 9-11 or JFK and suddenly you are a "conspiracy theorist".'

In the 1960s when Richard Hofstader wrote his famous essay, the perjorative power of 'conspiracy theorist' came from the association with the likes of the John Birch Society who believed that President Eisenhower was a part of the global communist conspiracy. These days the term gets its power from its association with the likes of David Icke who, notoriously, believes the world's elites are really extraterrestrial lizards disguised as the Queen, George Bush and so on; or the tens of thousands of Americans who apparently believe – as Icke used to before he discovered the lizards – that the world is run by a late 18th century secret society called the Illuminati.

I took LSD and other psychedelics in the 1970s and know how chemically precarious is that thing we call perceived reality. At their peak, the LSD microdots of the early 1970s dissolved visual reality. On the other hand, I live in the same world as everybody else: the kettle either boils or it doesn't. And this was true while I was trip-ping. At a meeting of philosophers around the turn of the century, Professor G. E. Moore gave a talk, 'Is their proof of an external world?' As the story was recounted to me by a philosopher tutor while I was at university, Moore walked to the podium and simply held out one hand and then another. Moore's gesture was a way of saying to the assembled philosophers: 'Some questions are not worth pursuing. There is a world outside myself, if the words "outside" and "myself" have any meaning.'

The world is what it is. We all agree upon what it is, most of the time and over most of our experience. At the edges of our collective experience the agreement breaks down.

Three years after Carl Oglesby's essay, 'In Defence of Paranoia', after more of the Watergate story had emerged, and President Nixon had resigned, the American writer, the late Ralph J. Gleason, formulated his First Law of American politics after Watergate: *No matter how paranoid you are, what the government is really doing is worse than you could possible imagine.*

Looking at the terrible world we live in, another joke from that period seems apt: I'm paranoid but am I paranoid enough?

Notes

1 Some people suspect the groups of dead sea mammals – dolphins, whales – which are washed-up on beaches around the world are the result of navies using extremely low frequency communications.

CONSPIRACIES . .

CHAPTER TWO

The Truth Behind the X-Files: Conspiracy Theories of the Failing American Empire

Edinburgh International Science Festival, 1997.

The current popularity of what is now known as the X-files agenda is amusing – and surprising – for the little group of us who have been keeping an eye on the crazy stuff on the fringe of our culture. What had previously been in the background – or underground – has suddenly leapt into the foreground. And there's little that's more foreground than The X-Files. There are now five or six professionally produced, full-colour, nationally distributed magazines devoted to The X-files agenda, which I would roughly define as the paranormal and conspiracy theories. This material has now penetrated large areas of popular American culture. In the recent movie The Rock, Sean Connery plays a British SAS officer who stole former FBI chief J. Edgar Hoover's secret files. The final scene of the film shows the Connery character's sidekick picking up the files, hidden by Connery years before. As he and his girlfriend drive off he holds up a strip of microfilm and says, 'Want to know who really killed Kennedy?'

One day someone will go back through the culture of the past thirty years and show in great detail how this change took place. Living in the UK, the landmarks on the paranormal side of the agenda seem to me to have been the following:

The book by Pauwels and Bergier, *The Dawn of Magic* or *The Morning of the Magicians*, its American title, first published in the UK in 1963. It was Pauwels and Bergier who brought to the mass audience the subjects of psychic powers, apparent links between the occult and the Nazi regime in Germany, UFOs, strange anomalies in the natural world, theories about the pyramids and so forth.

Second was the series of books by John Michell, most famously *The Flying Saucer Vision* in 1967, which introduced ley lines, geomancy, numerology, and extra-terrestrials – the whole earth mysteries thing. (How far we've come since then is suggested by the appearance on 23 March of an article in *The Sunday Telegraph* travel and tourism section on ley lines in England.)

The third landmark was the book *Psychic Discoveries Behind the Iron Curtain* by two *Reader's Digest* journalists in 1970 which appeared to show that the Soviet Union's government was funding research into psychic or paranormal phenomena. This was significant in that if a strictly materialist culture like the Soviet Union was taking the subject seriously, it was hard to argue, as most of science did in the West, that this was all mystical nonsense.

The fourth significant event was the emergence of Uri Geller and Matthew Manning in the early and mid 1970s – especially Geller, who appeared to demonstrate powers beyond the known laws of physics – and was doing it on television. I can still vividly remember Geller appearing on BBC. He took David Dimbleby's car key, stroked it, put it on the table and, as the camera zoomed in, like millions of other people, I saw that key continue to bend, untouched.

The fifth significant feature was people like Erich von Danniken who popularised much of this material with their tales of strange phenomena – Bermuda Triangle, pyramids, Space Gods and so forth.

Sixth, throughout this period, in the background then, was the UFO mystery which culminated in Spielberg's films *Close Encounters* in 1977 and then *ET*.

Seventh, in the mid 1980s a sudden burst of channelling – apparent communication with spirits – in the USA.

And eighth, in the late 1980s, more or less simultaneously, the emergence of anxieties about mind control – the state's alleged use of technology to control or manipulate its citizens – and the current explosion of UFO reports, stories of abductions, contacts, and landings by extraterrestrials.

Twenty years after *Close Encounters of the Third Kind*, The X-files program has taken that UFO material and added bits of everything else that was floating around on the fringes of science, mysticism and the paranormal. A virtual parallel world has been created.

The source materials for The X-files programs comes from catalogues like *Frontiers Science*, which offers books or video tapes on lost cities – MU, Atlantis, Lemuria – and a host of others in Africa, Central and South America. Without apparent anxiety, it offers five conflicting identifications and locations for Atlantis, including one claiming that Atlantis was the state of Wisconsin in the USA! It has cryptozoology: Big Foot, Sasquatch, Yeti; giants, sea monsters; crop circles here there and everywhere; Stonehenge and all the other stone architecture before Christ; extraterrestrial archaeology allegedly showing buildings on Mars and the Moon; antigravity devices; UFOs and aliens; free energy devices; Tesla technology; alternative science and treatments of every kind from cold fusion to radionics and Wilhelm Reich's orgone boxes; ley lines, earth mysteries; geomancy – and, the most recent addition to this collection, a section called conspiracy and secret societies in history.

It is against this background that the makers of The X-files and their derivatives like Dark Skies, have produced their programmes. These programmes are built on three primary elements:

1. An acceptance of what used to be described as the paranormal or psychic as real, routine, operational.
2. Distrust of the US central government: a willingness to believe it capable of great evil and great secrecy – in short that it is a conspiracy against its citizens.
3. In particular, the belief that there has been a massive US government cover-up of information on the UFO-alien subject; and, possibly, a cover-up of contact between extraterrestrial beings and officials of the US government.

These elements are brought together in Channel Four's Dark Skies which rewrites some of the major events of

US post-war history as if there had been an ongoing conspiracy between certain sections of the US government and aliens. At least that's what I think it contains: I have to confess I've never managed to sit through an entire episode of either Dark Skies or The X-Files.

Like everything else, from Coca-Cola to the ideology of New Labour, the conspiracy theories we're getting, those which make up the thematic background to the X Files and Dark Skies, are US imports This doesn't mean that there aren't conspiracy theories in other countries. There are a lot of conspiracy theories on the right of Japanese politics, for example, including some anti-semitic theories, even though there are no Jews in Japan. And there *is* an upsurge of anti-Jewish theories in the former Soviet Union and its empire; there were distinct anti-semitic tinges to Solidarity in Poland. In France Le Pen's National Front comes to mind. In Austria there are some pretty stinky people around the Freedom Party. The Arab world is still distributing the *Protocols of the Learned Elders of Zion* as if it was a real document. And so forth. But as far as Britain is concerned this conspiracy material is coming across the Atlantic. It is one of the bonuses of having been the unsinkable aircraft carrier for the US Armed Forces for the last 50 years.

America certainly is awash in conspiracy theories. Some people attribute this to PMT, pre-millennial tension. I don't think this is a very significant factor, though it has added a peculiarly millennial flavour to some of the conspiracy theorists on the American Christian fringe. (There are some examples in Kevin McClure's excellent *Fortean Times Book of the Millennium*.)

In my view the proliferation of conspiracy theories is attributable to more prosaic factors, and it's those I will discuss. It is the result of three things: the failing US empire; recent developments in reprographic and communication technologies; and the actual events in US political history since the sixties.

First the failing US empire. The American Dream is faltering. At best, real wage rates are no higher than they were twenty years ago for many of the working class in America. For many they are lower. There are thousands of homeless people on the streets of all the big American cities. The gap between the top strata in the US and the bottom is wider than it has been since the Second World War, and getting wider every year. In my view this is the predictable – and predicted – consequence of the infantile free market economic theories of the Reagan-Bush and Thatcher regimes; but whatever view is taken of the causes of this, things are not going according to plan for many white Americans, and they need to explain this to themselves.

You can see the change reflected in the US accounts of encounters with Extra Terrestrials. In the 1950s, when the US empire was booming, and the average white American consumer was experiencing increasing material prosperity, the extraterrestrials reportedly contacting the America citizen were largely benign. Now that the US empire is falling apart and sections of the big American cities are turning into war zones, the skies over America at night are apparently – *apparently* – bustling with Alien Rapists, beaming down into peoples' bedrooms to scoop them up and take them away for extended sessions of sexual abuse, forced copulation and experiments. In the 1950s white America had blue skies. Today they have dark skies.

Surveys regularly report that only around 2% of adult Americans read books of any kind. As you discover when you visit the place, most American newspapers and magazines barely mention the outside world, and the primary source of information for most Americans is television. But most American television simply does not deal with real political and economic issues in enough depth for the average American citizen to understand something as complicated as the economic decline of a great power.

The average American knows things are going wrong – but not why. Not only are the information and concepts they need not readily available, they are handicapped in their ability to understand the world by the power of the American myth. America, after all, is the country of manifest destiny, bearing the shining torch of freedom and democracy, the land of the brave and the home of the free. Most importantly and most damaging, America is a country in which anyone can make it and become rich if they try hard enough. So deeply ingrained is this American myth, most Americans simply find it impossible to believe that there is something wrong with their economic and social *system*. But if the *system* is fine, and things are going wrong what is causing the problem?

The answer is, of course, that things are going wrong because of the actions of . . . *bad people*. And not only must there be somebody to blame for their problems, they're doing it behind everybody's backs. This must be the case because most people can't see them doing it! The essence of the standard conspiracy theory is this: somebody's *behind* our troubles and behind the scenes.

Most conspiracy theories provide a simple explanation: things are going wrong because of X. Of course the X changes. Different groups are scapegoated. Since the 19th century the Freemasons, Catholics, and the Jews have been blamed by significant sections of the American population; and there were great anti-communist witch-hunts after each World War. There are obvious similarities between today's conspiracy theories portraying America threatened by extraterrestrial aliens, and the post WW1 and WW2 scares that aliens – immigrants from Europe, with socialist beliefs, after WW1; a secret network of communist agents after WW2 – were threatening America. It is also striking that the recent explosion of stories about alien abductions and UFO flaps in America have coincided with the collapse of the great Red Menace.

Most conspiracy theories come from white people. There are some distinctively black conspiracy theories: enough for an American academic to write a book about them a couple of years ago. Currently a large section of African Americans appear to believe that the CIA was deliberately selling crack cocaine to them to finance the war against Nicaragua. But American conspiracy theories seem to be primarily a white phenomenon; and primarily a white male phenomenon (though there are some prominent women); and primarily a working class or blue collar rather than middle or upper class male phenomenon. It may be simply that the middle class is too *educated* to believe the crazier large-scale conspiracy theories, and the upper classes too close to real power to believe them.

The second factor in the rapid spread of conspiracy theories is technology. When I first became aware of US conspiracy theories in the 1970s, the type-generating Apple Mac and the FAX had not been invented, photocopiers were expensive machines which still used rolls of coated paper, and newspapers and magazines were still set in metal type. In those days the amateur publication looked like an amateur publication. It was simply too expensive to make it look professional. These days about £500, maybe less, will buy a second-hand computer kit with which it is possible to make your copy look like *The Times*, if you want to. And there are fax machines, cheap telephones and, most of all the internet. Today, for a relatively small outlay, almost anybody can put their theories up on the internet and wait for people to browse through them, pick them up and pass them on. Any old nonsense gets posted on the net. To some extent, the spread of conspiracy theories has been brought about by communication technology. Even I've got a website.

The third, and I think most important factor is a shift that has taken place in our perception of the real world;

behind conspiracy theories are real events. In 1963, conspiracy theorists as we now think of them were a tiny minority in both Britain and America whose views were rarely if ever reported in the mass media of the day. In 1964 an American journalist came to Britain and surveyed what he called in the title of the subsequent book, *The British Political Fringe*. On the far right he found the neo-nazis, Oswald Mosley, and the League of Empire Loyalists, a little group semi-detached from the right of the Tory Party. All of these groups believed in variants of the Jewish conspiracy theory; that is that the Jews controlled the world's financial system. But their combined membership was only a few thousand. In America at the same time, there was the US Nazi Party, some racists groups in the southern states such as the States Rights Party, and the John Birch Society. The latter was most famous – or notorious – for the claim by its founder that President Eisenhower was a conscious agent of the communist conspiracy. Of these US groups, the Birchers, as they were known, were the most signifi-cant with two congressmen who were associated with them.

The shift began in the 1960s. And no wonder. Amer-ican history since the 60s has been a long succession of assassinations and conspiracies. Their three most impor-tant left of centre politicians, the Kennedy brothers and Martin Luther King, were assassinated – none of them by the assassin identified by the authorities. Much of the leadership of the Black Panthers was murdered – and it was revealed a decade later, largely as a result of a conspiracy by the FBI. Then came Watergate and the various revelations trailing in its wake of widespread surveillance and covert operations by the FBI and the CIA. And there was the war in Vietnam. After 1980 began the various intelligence, military, and financial scandals – conspiracies – of the Reagan-Bush era, of which the secret financing of the war against the Nicaraguan government by illegally selling arms to Iran was just the most prominent. In other words, from the assassinations of the 1960's through to Iran-Contra and the other Reagan-Bush horrors in the 1980s, events have revealed major governmental conspiracies which have made it impossible for the powers-that-be to maintain the line that such things just don't happen.

Chris Carter, the writer/producer of The X-files TV program commented recently that his perception of the United States was formed by Watergate. But I think the key event was the killing of John Kennedy, and the refusal of a handful of stubborn Americans to accept the official government line that Lee Harvey Oswald did it. If anybody is to be credited with the current mess we're in, it's those critics of the Warren Commission. Resisting all the government propaganda, personal vilification and manipulation of the media, their persistence destroyed the government's case, and made the first big hole in the official version of America. From their research grew knowledge of the CIA and other US secret organisations; and without that knowledge the US media would not have known enough to investigate Watergate; and from there to do more investigations of the CIA etc.

50 years of secrecy, lies, media manipulation and covert operations are coming back to bite the legs of the elite managers of American society and politics. A large number of US citizens no longer believe government statements about anything; and a significant minority believe the federal government capable of any calumny, up to and including planning to brainwash its citizenry, detonating the bomb in Oklahoma to give itself a pretext for pushing draconian anti-terrorism laws through Congress, and even organising a secret conspiracy with extraterrestrial beings begun in the late 1940s.

In retrospect it became absurd to deny the reality of large-scale conspiracies in Western democracies when the activities of the CIA began to be revealed in the early 1960s. Yet despite that, and despite the history of America since then, for most of the Anglo-American chattering classes – the media, academics, politicians – to be labelled a 'conspiracy theorist' is the kiss of death. One of the bed-rocks of the ideology of liberal democracies like ours remains that conspiracy theories are always wrong, and those who espouse them are mental incompetents. This belief usually manifests itself in statements like this: 'Of course I'm not a believer in the conspiracy theory of history'; or 'As usual, the cock-up theory of politics turned out to be true'. Belief in the cock-up or coincidence theory of history is at the heart of what passes for political and intellectual sophistication in liberal democracies.

This is understandable up to a point. Who wants to be associated with nutters who believe the world's being run by a cabal of American politicians and extraterrestrials from a bunker under the desert in New Mexico? Or who believe that the Queen controls the world's heroin trade and was responsible for the assassination of John Kennedy, as do followers of Lyndon La Rouche? However, this legitimate allergy to dotty conspiracy *theories* extends much further than the crazy fringe to a general prohibition on conspiracies *per se*. And this is very strange, because, even ignoring all the evidence of large-scale political conspiracies, and organisations such as intelligence agencies which are conspiracies pure and simple, it is blindingly obvious, is it not, that political parties, for example, are intrinsically conspiratorial. Routine internal party politics is a network of inter-locking cabals plotting how to get their hands on this group, committee, caucus meeting, council, party, pressure group. The squabbles in the Tory Party in Scotland, reported this week, illustrate this perfectly, do they not? It is only a slight exaggeration to say, as the American writer Carl Oglesby did in the early 1970s, that conspiracy *is* normal politics. Yet this idea would produce everything from outrage to patronising shakes of the head from almost all intellectual and political circles in this country. The well modulated Oxbridge tones would say; 'Really, old boy, the world just isn't like that.'

The belief that our society *just isn't like that* is intrinsic to the concept of pluralism at the heart of the ideology of liberal democracy. This is mostly what's taught in the politics departments of Anglo-American universities. The last time I took a look at it, British academic politics was still wrestling with the discovery that interest and pressure groups intrude into the model of Westminster party politics. Pluralism says many groups have some power in society. Basically, that's all. But the problem with 'pluralism' is that it is essentially empty. The interesting questions begin where pluralism stops. Which groups? How much power?

A rational perspective, what I would call a parapolitical perspective, on the other hand, takes it for granted that there are clandestine influences – conspiracies – at work in society. Not the ridiculous, world-controlling conspiracies like the Freemasons, or the Illuminati, or President Harry Truman meets the aliens, but more mundane things like intelligence agencies manipulating domestic and international politics; companies buying government policies by making anonymous donations to the Tory Party and so forth.

Simple empirical observation shows conspiracy to be a very common form of political behaviour. The mysterious thing is not that some poor deluded fools insist on seeing conspiracies, but how it is that, for so long, so many otherwise apparently intelligent people – most of Anglo-American political science, for example – have managed not to notice that conspiracy is an everyday and rather important part of the subject they purport to be studying. Let me give a couple of examples.

Since its formation in the 1920s until its demise about 6 years ago, the Economic League collected and spent, in today's money, millions of pounds every year working against the British Left. It may have spent as much as the

Conservative Party since WW1. Yet there was not one academic essay about the Economic League between its formation and 1980. Not one in sixty years. No account of British domestic politics in the 20th century can be anything but hopelessly incomplete without incorporating the Economic League, but I have never seen one that does.[1]

Academic American history somehow manages to skip over the fact that in a five year period in the sixties, one president, the probable next president, and the most important black leader since the war were victims of assassinations which were never investigated properly and remain unsolved.

It is not difficult to explain why this odd situation has prevailed for so long. Britain has been run for most of this century by two intensely secretive, overlapping groups; one is the British state, about which we know very little – especially its secret branches about which even MPs are not allowed to ask questions. An MP may not even ask a Parliamentary question about the security and intelligence services; the clerks in the House of Commons will simply refuse to accept such questions. The other is the Conservative Party, whose funding is still a secret. Here we are, approaching the millennium, and we still do not know who is funding one of our major political parties. In the US, since the war, a group of government agencies, with their satellite supply companies, headed by the CIA and the Pentagon, have been operating largely in secret, spending about 50% of the US budget – and very profitably, too. It's often difficult to show the links between ideology on the one hand and material interests on the other, but in these cases it looks pretty straightforward to me. The most powerful interests in Britain and the US don't want their conspiratorial activities examined; and, surprise surprise, it turns out that being interested in conspiracies is intellectually forbidden in both societies.

There's one obvious exception to the official prohibition on interest in conspiracies. Since 1918 we have all been officially encouraged to believe in the existence of one conspiracy: the Red Menace. In Britain until recently, the most significant conspiracy theorists were the Cold War warriors, many of them employed by the state, who churned out the endless tales of Soviet espionage and subversion since the Second World War – indeed, since the First World War. Mrs Thatcher believed all this. She looked at the Trades Union Congress, at Uncle Jack Jones, one of the nicest and most decent people who ever existed, and saw Moscow subversion. And to ensure that we believed in the reality of this approved conspiracy theory, the Anglo-American intelligence services – some of the outstanding examples of institutionalised conspiracies in the 20th century – have spent a ton of money propagating it, while denigrating anybody who turned up with any other kind of conspiracy. This hypocrisy reached some kind of peak in 1969 when the CIA – a vast world-wide conspiracy if ever there was one – put out a message to all its stations and personnel about the Kennedy assassination. The instruction from CIA HQ was that they were to use their political and media assets to put out the line that the kind of scenario described by the Kennedy assassination conspiracy theorists could not possibly exist! Who better to put out a 'no conspiracy' message than one of the biggest conspiracies of the post-war era!

Intelligence agencies – the secret arms of the state – have been among the chief generators of conspiracy theories since World War 2. One of the unfortunate skills acquired during the war was black propaganda; and with the onset of the Cold War both sides began churning out disinformation about their opponents, much of it delivered to contested areas in the developing world. For example: employees of the US and Israeli governments, with assistance from some British personnel, invented and spread the conspiracy theory that the KGB, using the Bulgarians, shot the present Pope in 1981. A former CIA station chief no less, Paul Henze, wrote the first book articulating this nonsense; and the theme was taken up enthusiastically by other CIA assets, including the journalist the late Claire Sterling. In retaliation, the Soviets invented and spread the conspiracy theory that AIDS was a biological weapon developed by the US army designed to kill people of colour.

To take another example, in the wake of the Kennedy assassination both the Soviet and French intelligence services put out conspiracy theories about the killing; the Soviets spreading their disinformation blaming the CIA through an Italian newspaper and thence into a French-language Canadian paper, and thence into the JFK researchers. The French published a book, a famous book in the JFK world, called *Farewell America*. Both blamed the CIA for the shooting.

This aspect of the Cold War has yet to be looked at in any detail, but my guess would be that we will eventually discover that quite substantial chunks of what we thought was history has been faked.

But how do we tell which conspiracy theories are worth taking seriously? Take UFOs. It is now preposterous to deny the existence of UFOs: there are too many reliable witnesses, too many bits of film and videotape from all over the world. But from there to the Alien Sex Fiend Abduction stories is an enormous step. UFO's remain just that: *Unidentified* Flying Objects. That they exist cannot be rationally denied. But to go beyond that, it gets pretty iffy, pretty quickly. There is no evidence that I am aware of, for the existence of aliens. No artefacts, no photographs, no film or videotape.

Nonetheless behind a surprising number of the bizarre stories sitting out there on the internet, there is something – maybe just a fragment – which is real.

Sometimes even the most implausible claim has to be taken seriously. For over twenty years a handful of people have claimed that the US never went to the moon. It was all faked in a movie studio, they said, a large-scale piece of political propaganda in the Cold War with the Russians. The film Capricorn One, with one O.J. Simpson among its cast, dealt with this. In one version of this theory, it was all faked in a studio and directed by Stanley Kubrick. He, after all, had just directed the film 2001: if anyone had shown they could fake a moon landing, it was he. At first glance this is just profoundly implausible – stupid, really. A conspiracy that big would involve hundreds, maybe thousands of people keeping quiet for decades. It just couldn't be done, could it? Somebody would talk; somebody would sell the story to the media for big bucks. But – even here there is a but – a photographic expert is now claiming that some of the photographs given out by NASA as shots of the moon landings were done in a studio. There was a long, careful, and I think totally convincing analysis published in *The Fortean Times* about six months ago. But, even if true, what does this suggest? Do fake pictures mean a fake moon-landing? More likely, surely, that NASA just dummied some up on earth; you get better pictures in a studio than on the moon. And NASA wanted maximum publicity to enable it to screw maximum dollars out of Congress. In a studio, for example, you can spotlight the US flag on the otherwise rather dimly-lit lunar module . . . And so, 25 years later, a sharp-eyed photographer thinks, hang on a minute: on the moon there is only one source of light, so where has the spotlight come from?

On the whole, the smaller the event allegedly explained by a conspiracy theory, the more likely it is to be worth taking seriously. A government agency out of control; a plot to raise money for the Contras after Congress cut off its funds; an assassination or two. The investigation of such theories, conspiracy research, what has been termed parapolitics, takes the simple, official account of reality and makes the world more complex. For example, 300 books and half a dozen journals on the

Kennedy assassination – not to mention perhaps a million declassified pages of FBI and CIA materials on the subject – have destroyed the simple 1964 Warren Commission conclusion that the 'lone nut' did it, and have generated immense complexity on the details surrounding the event. And this is replicated in most of the big issues of the last twenty years. The public documentation on the Iran-Contra affair, for example, is now vast.

But as soon as conspiracy theories attempt to encompass wider events – the Russian revolution was the work of Freemasons, or Jews or Wall St bankers, for example – they become less likely. These mega- or macro-conspiracy theories *simplify* reality. The chaos of the world's economic system is reduced to a cabal of Jewish bankers. The US were in Vietnam because of the heroin in the Golden Triangle. The Freemasons are running British politics. This simplification is undoubtedly the appeal of mega-conspiracy theories to some people. The world's ills are explained by the actions of this or that group – or individual; all the difficult, time-consuming complexity of real life, and real politics, can be ignored.

Mega-conspiracy theories are simply bad theories, held irrationally, in the face of the evidence which falsifies them. Lyndon LaRouche has no evidence that the Queen runs the world's heroin traffic. There is no evidence that a secret cabal called the Illuminati have been running the world since the late 18th century. There is no evidence that the world's financial system is controlled by Jewish bankers. There is no evidence of a

US government-alien conspiracy which began in the late 1940s.

These mega-conspriacy theories are amusing – but they are also a menace. For they enable the powers-that-be to dismiss people like me along with the people who believe that the Jews, the Illuminati, or aliens are running the world. Yes, conspiracies are real; and yes, they are important. But there isn't just one big overarching conspiracy; there are thousands of smaller conspiracies, many of them competing, interlocking, overlapping. Lee Harvey Oswald had clear connections to the FBI and the CIA; Jack Ruby was an FBI informant in the early 1950s and the payoff man between organised crime and the Dallas Police. So when Ruby shot Oswald, all these organisations had reasons to cover-up the truth about their connections to them. There *was* a conspiracy to murder Kennedy but there were many conspiracies after his death to suppress the truth and mislead the investigations which had nothing to do with the initial assassination conspiracy.

The importance of the concept of conspiracy is political. As well as being what the Marxist left would call a naive empiricist, I am also a naive democrat. I believe that the political process should be open, transparent. I don't like secrecy, and that means I don't like conspiracies. Be it Trotskyist groups inside the Labour Party; be it companies bribing governments; be it MI5 and Special Branch in the green and anti-roads movements – and the Scots Nats – trying to conjure up a new enemy to keep themselves in a job. The importance of the notion of conspiracy, is the way it reminds us of how much of this society operates in secret; how far this is from being a democratic society controlled by its citizens. The garbage of which we are now getting so much, the global conspiracy baloney, is simply background noise, a distraction. Anthony Summers, the British investigator and writer, summed up the position very well: he said he wasn't interested in conspiracy *theories*, but he was interested in theories *about* conspiracies.

In this country – I mean Britain, not Scotland – the conspiracies we should be looking at are those run by the auld enemies: the state, especially the secret state, and its allies in the Conservative Party and the mass media; and big capital. The usual suspects, in other words, not the current X-files agenda, fascinating though some of it undoubtedly is.

Notes

1 To my knowledge, general histories of this country's politics still do not include anything about the Economic League; but in the last 25 years there has been a good deal of research, mostly on the left, into the organisation. It apparently went bust in 1993 but a remnant organisation called Caprim carried on. The current status of Caprim and its function of monitoring 'subversives' at work is unclear.

CHAPTER THREE

9/11 and Iraq

Leeds Stop the War Group, 2002.

This talk is the only one I have given on 9/11. When I finished and the chair asked for contributions from the floor, the first comment was from a young Muslim woman who told the meeting that the Jews in the World Trade Centre building had been told not to come to work that day. I tried but failed to persuade her that this was an urban myth. Some people – maybe most people – prefer myths to facts.

I was asked to talk about 9/11 and Iraq. I guess I was thought qualified to talk about 9/11 because I had an article on it published about 6 months ago in *Fortean Times*. But I'm a generalist and while I did spend some weeks collecting and trying to organise the torrent of information about 9/11 which was appearing in the event's aftermath, I moved on to other areas. And about Iraq I probably know less than many of the people in this room. You get my drift here: I am trying to reduce your expectations.

What I have written is a sketch, a framework, which I hope will provoke a discussion, rather than a lecture. Talking with people is more interesting than talking to or at people.

So I'll start with 9/11. When I sat down to think about this I began rummaging through my computer and found I had tried to write about 9/11 on four occasions before the *Fortean Times* article, each time giving up because the material was too complicated to handle except at extreme length. This first section is based on the beginning of something I wrote between 9/11 2001 and November 2001 – in other words, while the subject was in the forefront of our minds.

On the day of the plane bombings, an American with the e-mail moniker Top-view, told the people on his distribution list that the World Trade Centre attacks had been the work of what he called the BushMob. He wrote:

'So many of the BushMob's high-priority agendas are furthered by this morning's events that it's just not possible they were not the original and primary motivators of the monstrous devastation wrought in New York City.'

'Top-view' called it the American Reichstag Fire. As did the veteran conspiracy theorist Sherman Kolnick, in one of his commentaries on the event two days later. As did the Russian writer, Boris Kagarlitsky, writing in *Moscow Times* on 18 September.

On 13 September a website carried what purported to be a tape-recording of a phone-call made from a US aircraft carrier, before the bombings, which spoke of 'something big' about to happen in the US. This produced the following conclusion, the basic thesis spelt out in simple terms:

'. . . the Bush Administration wanted a massive, earth-shaking act of terrorism unleashed upon a major U.S. metropolitan area, in order to generate and galvanise support among the people for implementation of martial law conditions within the territory of the United States,

and drastic, severe curtailment of Constitutional rights and civil liberties.'

On the same day, 13 September, Israeli sources announced that Iraq was probably behind the events and someone called roadsafetycrew with the e-mail address <@orwellian.org> claimed:

'NBC news reports the Iraqi embassy – apparently somewhere near the White House and Pentagon – tried to take out a massive insurance policy in the days before the attack. The insurance company contacted the State Department to verify it wouldn't violate embargo restrictions.'

Rushing to judgement, two well known names in the Kennedy assassination world broadcast their speculations on the event in the first week. John Judge, who runs COPA, the Committee on Political Assassinations, wrote:

'The non-response [by the US Air Force] as the Dulles plane flew over the White House and turned to go into the Pentagon is inexplicable that late in the scenario unless this was in inside job. I am sure there is a false sponsor ready to be handed to us.'

And this was the writer Jim Marrs, who has written books on the Kennedy assassination and the UFO mystery:

'But one thing appears quite clear, the tragic events of 9-11 play right into the hands of persons with an agenda

aimed at eroding American liberties and sovereignty . . .
No matter who was speaking, their "party line" was the
same: terrible tragedy, find and punish those responsible,
stop terrorism. But, of course, since terrorists move
between national boundaries, we must join with other
"freedom loving" nations and work with the United
Nations and NATO to combat this new menace. This is a
thinly-disguised effort to have a mourning and emotional
American public stampeded into their New World Order.'

The basic thought in these minds was: this is so convenient for the Bush government, it really stinks. Remember
on September 10, 2001 the American media and political
system had not yet forgotten that the Republicans had just
stolen the 2001 American election; their little coup in
Florida, with the support from a Republican-supporting
Supreme Court. Bush was not legitimate on 9/11.

Once the possibility that 9/11 was a stunt was
admitted, little oddities began to be seen in the first
reports. This appeared the day after:

'BOSTON (Reuters) – Investigators in Boston found a
copy of the Koran, a videotape on how to fly commercial
jets and a fuel consumption calculator in a pair of bags
meant for American Airlines Flight 11, which crashed
into the World Trade Center on Tuesday, the 'Boston
Globe' reported on Wednesday. The paper said the suit-
cases belonged to a man with an Arabic name who
investigators believe was one of those who hijacked the
plane and crashed it into the New York landmark. The

man boarded Flight 11 after flying into Boston's Logan
International airport from Portland, Maine, but his bags
missed the connection, the 'Globe' reported.'

The *Boston Herald* reported on its website, citing an
unidentified source, that 'Massachusetts authorities have
identified five Arab men as suspects in the attacks and
have seized a rental car containing Arabic-language
flight training manuals at Logan.'

Our hijackers are leaving very loud clues everywhere:
the Koran, flight manuals. Could hardly be more
obvious. For people like Marrs and John Judge – and for
me – this had a familiar ring to it. I noted at the time:
'Thus began the discovery of the most comprehensive
paper trail left behind after a major crime since James
Earl Ray allegedly dropped a bag next to the crime scene
with his name on some of the items.'

James Earl Ray was framed for the murder of Martin
Luther King. Central to the prosecution was a bag of
personal effects found in a doorway near the scene of the
crime, which contained clothes, some of which had his
name on them. This seemed a little obvious. For those
with suspicions about the incident, the Koran and the
flight training manuals seemed a little obvious.

On the 21 September someone called Sam Yousef,
noted that all four of the apparently indestructible
aircraft 'black boxes' had been destroyed, yet one of the
hijackers' passports had been found in the rubble of the
WTC buildings. He asked: 'What kind of idiots does the
FBI take us for?'

Again: the passport find was a little obvious. The paper trail apparently left behind by the hijackers was sufficiently surprising for even George Monbiot to raise his eyebrows at it in his *Guardian* column on 16 October.

The story of the passport 'found' in the smouldering rubble of the Twin Towers, of Mohammed Atta, was reported by CNN. I found their report on their website in September but it has since been deleted.

Other items have been deleted from websites. The website of the Andrews Air Force, from which, in the normal course of events, planes would have taken off to investigate the hijacked airliners, was closed and reopened having been rewritten.

Another little event which fuelled the conspiracy buffs was the curious tale of the demolition expert who changed his mind. By the second day a number of correspondents were expressing doubt about the fall of the towers and someone noticed that in the *Albuquerque Journal* in New Mexico, on the day of the attacks, an article had appeared quoting a New Mexico-based demolition expert, Van Romero, which began thus: 'Televised images of the attacks on the World Trade Center suggest that explosive devices caused the collapse of both towers, a New Mexico Tech explosion expert said Tuesday.' Three weeks later it was noticed that not only had a piece been published noting that Van Romero had changed his mind, the *Albuquerque Journal* had altered their web page for 9/11, removing their original story and putting Romero's recantation in its place.

I'm not going to try and make the case for a US government conspiracy. I don't believe that's what happened. I offer these examples – a sample of many – really as a kind of flavour of the thinking of the people, on the Internet – Americans mostly – who, while the Twin Towers were still smouldering, had already concluded that it was a fake, a con, a deception, designed to allow the American national security state to bring in repressive legislation at home and pursue wars abroad.

And it has to be acknowledged that about domestic repression, the paranoids were right: a hi-tech, authoritarian, militaristic state is being created. American librarians are facing legislation which will make them monitor their readers' choice of reading material. American airline companies now have a list of a thousand people – most of them American; radicals of one stripe or another – who are now regarded as potentially dangerous. The Net is now carrying reports from environmentalists, anti-globalisation protesters reporting that they are being strip-searched at airports.

About foreign wars, the paranoids were right. Here comes Iraq and the never-ending, all-encompassing 'war on terror'.

Never mind for the moment that 24 hours after 9/11 there was no evidence that it was a hoax, it was startling to read more or less rational people argue that the US government – or the US state – was prepared to murder thousands of its citizens and do serious damage to its financial centre in pursuit of policy objectives. Since then there has developed a huge body of work, almost all of it on the Net, trying to substantiate that initial gut reaction while watching the Twin Towers fall. On Saturday, I asked the Google search engine for '9/11, conspiracy' and got 11,00 hits.

I've looked at a tiny fraction of those and yes, of course, most of it is crap; but there is a core which isn't; or, at any rate, isn't obviously crap. The anomalous reports I quoted above are just the tip of a substantial iceberg. Gore Vidal covered this much better than I could in *The Observer* a few weeks ago; and if you missed it, it is on the Net.

As well as the hard core who think that the CIA or the Pentagon or the Israeli intelligence service Mossad did 9/11, there is a wider group who think that while the US national security state – the CIA, perhaps – didn't organise this, they knew it was going to happen. A group of relatives of the 9/11 victims is now suing the US government, for, as they put it, allowing it to happen on purpose. This tells us that at least one American lawyer thinks there is enough evidence for this to be worth some of his or her time.

The hard core who assumed from the outset that it was a phoney, are part of a relatively new phenomenon, a conspiracy subculture which is difficult to assign to Right or Left. In the 1980s, the traditional Left-Right divide began to blur a little in America. In the 1970s, it was people on the American Left who began looking at the policy groupings of American and American-dominated capital: the Council on Foreign Relations and trans-national groups like the Trilateral Commission and Bilderberg group. The best book I know on the Council on Foreign Relations was published by that most venerable of American Marxist journals, *The Monthly Review*. There is a well known book edited by Holly Sklar, *Trilateralism*, published in 1980. In the early 1980s, people like me bought it. For the last decade, to Sklar's reported distress, it has almost exclusively been bought by the Right, by what we might call the New World Order theorists, who range from pretty serious researchers to the people who believe the UN is on the verge of taking over the United States and warn their readers to watch out for those UN troops in their blue berets!

You get a hint of how this overlapping of Left and Right happened from the subtitle of Sklar's book: 'The Trilateral commission and Elite Planning for World Management.' *Elite* planning . . . Though I don't suppose Sklar intended it, 'elite' was a key term among the conspiracy theorists of the Right. They might not all agree on which elite was secretly running the Federal Reserve, debauching the currency, running America into the ground and preparing to hand it over to the New World Order, but they were all agreed it was an *elite*. Not the people.

In the late 1960s, it was the radical Left who began writing of Amerika, with a K instead of the C. In the 1990s, it was a section of the radical Christian Right which claimed to see an American Reich being created by the Clinton administration and the federal government; and some of them began to spell America with a K. And what happened? The Feds confirmed their worst imaginings at Ruby Ridge and Waco, Texas, treating a family in the backwoods and a fringe Christian group as if they were terrorists and killing over 80 of them. Cue the American militia movement.

As the Right in the 1980s and 90s embraced items from what had been a Left agenda, some on the American Left took fright and began to distance themselves from the Right – and any talk of conspiracy. There is almost nothing the Left fears more than being associated in some way with the Right. We are dealing with concepts and psychological forces here such as purity and contamination.

The major media noticed this apparent crossover and it was described as fusion paranoia . . . Of course the degree of fusion was slight, in fact, but the description was a splendid piece of psywar, bundling Left and Right together and labelling them both as 'paranoid'.

This conspiracy subculture looked at the post-war history of America:

- the rise of the corporations;
- the murderous foreign policy;
- the assassination of domestic politicians – JFK, King et al;
- the constant stream of political scandals involving the National Security State;
- the rise of increasing authoritarian federal bureaucracies – the murder of the 80 Branch Davidians at Waco, Texas, looms large;
- the useless, co-opted American media; and concluded that it is *all* a conspiracy:

- all politicians are bent, corrupted, agents of some intelligence agency or foreign country, or are being blackmailed;
- all the major media are corrupt;
- all received versions of reality are false.

It is this conspiracist subculture, which has been growing rapidly since the late 1980s, which assumed the US government or state had done 9/11. And part of the reason it assumed this is that it knew the US government and state had done some similar things before. Not as dramatic, maybe, but similar.

Some of this subculture believes that the Japanese were allowed, even encouraged, to attack Pearl Harbour to enable Roosevelt to take America into a war he had promised not to join. Another section of this subculture believes that at the Gulf of Tonkein in 1964, a North Vietnamese attack on US ships was fabricated to provide the pretext for LBJ to step up the war. In my view the Gulf of Tonkein story is true, the deception has been more or less admitted, and the Pearl Harbour story unproven.

After 9/11 the conspiracist subculture was enormously encouraged by the discovery and subsequent distribution on the net, three months after 9/11, of certain sections from a then recent book by James Bamford about the National Security Agency, NSA. These were extracts from declassified documents from the 1960s which show that in 1961/2 the Pentagon was trying to find a way to reinvade Cuba. The key problem they faced was finding a suitable pretext for the invasion.

Having no such pretext the Pentagon planners began thinking of ways to create one; and among the options being proposed was the creation of a phoney Cuban terror campaign. This included, and I quote:

'We could blow up a US ship and blame Cuba.'

'We could develop a Communist Cuba terror campaign in the Miami area, in other Florida cities and even in Washington. The terror campaign could be pointed at Cuban refugees seeking haven in the United States.We could sink a boatload of Cubans en route to Florida (real or simulated).' [1]

The idea of your own government, or state, killing thousands of its citizens seems less outrageous when you learn that 40 years before, the same institutions had been considering killing a few dozen in pursuit of something as relatively piffling as retaking Cuba. Same idea; only the scale is different.

I never took the US-did-it thesis seriously, even after Bamford's documents became available, because of the targets: Manhattan and the Pentagon. I just can't imagine them deciding to attack those. Had it been Disneyland, or some provincial city, I might have considered it. But not those towers of capital and their protector, the Pentagon. Too many friends and relatives might be involved; and why targets so big when the same effect on public opinion could have been generated by something less extravagant and less damaging to the US economy?

I'm with this conspiracist subculture part of the way.
Their reading of post-war US history is largely accurate.
Like them, I have seen the list of countries bombed by
the US government since the Second World War, 27 so
far; like them I have followed the big scandals, from
JFK's assassination through Iran-Contra etc. But I – and
I guess you – would use language they mostly wouldn't
– which tells us that most of the this subculture *hasn't*
come from the Left.

Bombing 27 countries since World War 2 is called
imperialism.

The evidence gathered by the conspiracists on 9/11
does not suggest to me that the US organised it or
allowed it to happen; but it does suggest that the US
intelligence community knew that Al-Qaeda was planning something big, but not precisely what, and decided
that this might be rather a handy pretext for the attack on
Afghanistan the US was planning.

To give just one example: *The Daily Telegraph* on-line
carried on the 16 September 2001, 5 days after, a story
with the headline 'Israeli security issued urgent warning
to CIA of large-scale terror attacks' which began:

> 'Israeli intelligence officials say that they warned their
> counterparts in the United States last month that large-
> scale terrorist attacks on highly visible targets on the
> American mainland were imminent. 'The Telegraph' has
> learnt that two senior experts with Mossad, the Israeli
> military intelligence service, were sent to Washington in
> August to alert the CIA and FBI to the existence of a cell

*of as many as 200 terrorists said to be preparing a big
operation.'*

And there are dozens of similar reports. It might be
noted that most of the sources the conspiracists are citing
in their theories are mainstream.

That the US was planning to attack Afghanistan before
9/11 was broadcast on the BBC World Service on 18
September, 2001, a week after 9/11; the source of the
story being a former Pakistani Foreign Minister.

In one of the Al-Qaeda documents published since
9/11 it is suggested that Al-Qaeda knew of the prepara-
tions to attack Afghanistan from a source in the Pakistan
government, and while never quite admitting that they
did 9/11, they hint that they were just getting their retaliation in first.

The evidence suggesting US foreknowledge of something big coming down the pipeline is a large number of
warnings delivered to the US from round the world,
sources up to President Putin of Russia; and the futures
speculation in the shares of certain companies directly
affected by the plane bombings just before 9/11. When
these futures contracts were discovered, the stock
exchanges in America, London and Hamburg all promised investigations; to date not a word has been
forthcoming from them.

But does speculation in the shares of, say, airline
companies imply foreknowledge of 9/11, or foreknowledge of, say, a hijacking which would in itself depress
the share values of airlines?

In the explosion of data which followed 9/11, a great deal of hitherto largely unnoticed information about US military and economic expansion into regions near Afghanistan became available; and with this came information on the oil politics behind these policies. This information-gathering and dissemination has been so widespread – again mostly through the Net – that almost no-one outside America believes that the planned attack on Iraq is about anything but oil.

And it is mostly but not entirely about oil. 9/11 gave us the 'war on terror' created by the US government as a reason – a pretext – for another imperialist push into the sphere of influence of the former Soviet Union. One imperial power replacing another. The Baltic states are to join NATO; the US is building military bases around the Caspian Sea. All of this was going to happen anyway; the planning and history is there to see. 9/11 just made it easier to stampede the opposition in Congress and the American media.

Harold Pinter gave a wonderful summary of US foreign policy: kiss my ass or I'll kick your head in. But this is the way all great powers behave. In 1880 or so, Palmerstone would have sent a gunboat to threaten Johnny Foreigner. The Soviets sent tanks. These days it's cruise missiles and B52s.

Same old same old in a sense; but with the new wrinkle: the US cannot afford many casualties. There is a distinct shortfall of young men willing to die for their country and there has been since the Korean War.

America is preparing to attack Iraq; and it's about oil. Without oil the US wouldn't be interested in Iraq. Why does the US want the oil? Because it ceased to be self-sufficient in oil in 1976; and because its society depends on high oil consumption.

This is obvious of course; one of the basic building blocks. But that oil dependency is only real when you get there. First time I visited the US was in 1993 and petrol in New Mexico was 97 cents – about 60p a gallon. In the UK it was heading towards £3.00. But without cheap energy there wouldn't be near universal air conditioning; and without air conditioning most of New Mexico, along with most of the entire South West of the US – and New York – would be almost unliveable in the summer. At any rate, life as it is currently lived would be impossible. In the Northern states, winters may last 6 months, sub zero temperatures for months at a time; life as it is lived would be impossible without cheap heating oil. The whole society is based on the car and cheap energy to an extent that I understood as an abstraction but didn't really grasp until my partner filled the large tank on our car for less than ten dollars in a petrol station in the Rockies. And it simply isn't practical politics in America to suggest that this should change. Ralph Nader, who does know this has to change, got two percent of the vote at the last Presidential election.

The Americans are going to destroy the planet, they are going fuck everybody – white, brown, yellow, black, pink – to get their hands on the world's oil. This is the forseeable geopolitical future. Iraq next – unless the

Americans run another, better organised coup in Venezuela before it. Ultimately, they will need the oil of the former Soviet Union. They're already circling round it, erecting a chain of military bases through the former southern Soviet republics, Uzbekistan, Kyrgyzstan, and Tajikistan.

How do we sell reducing their standard of living to the American middle class? This is the scale of the problem the world has. The Americans cannot be persuaded, cannot be argued, cannot be reasoned to surrender their standard of living. It will have to be taken off them. At one level let's try to 'prevent the war in Iraq'; at another, we need many Iraqs. America will have to be defeated, and repeatedly defeated. It is going to be very ugly indeed.

B following A may not mean that A caused B. There would have been an American attack on Iraq with or without al-Qaeda's attack on New York. But that has made it easier. Most Americans don't know where Iraq is and could not care less; Iraq, Iran, Saudi Arabia – they're somewhere over there and they're against the American way. Americans are profoundly provincial and parochial. There are no national media. There are regional and local media. What is being done in Washington is of almost no interest 2000 thousand miles away in rural America and they know nothing about it. And most of America is rural. I've done the road trip round the South Western states and Americans are lovely people but don't know anything about the rest of the world. All that stuff is true. For most of them, the information simply isn't presented in the major media.

Why this has happened sociologically – the underlying cause – I think is the decline in the standard of living of (white) American citizens as the so-called 'free market' in America redistributes from middle to top. Most Americans have no access to, nor have been accustomed to using, the kind of concepts with which to explain their declining standard of living and the chaos in their inner cities. What they do have access to and can handle is a kind of nativist, conspiratorial discourse – if I can use that word without evoking the dreaded postmodernists – in which the question that is asked is not: what is the explanation for this? But: who is responsible for this? Who is *behind* this? It remains to be seen if the experience in the last couple of years with Enron and the rest of it, the discovery that the banking and investment system appears to be designed to steal their savings, begins to shift the focus of attention onto structural questions. In my casual browsing through the conversations of the American populist Right on these issues, there seem to be faint signs of a light dawning that all may not be well with the American social and economic system – despite manifest destiny, and it being God's own country, the land of the brave and the home of the free.

Notes

1 The documents from which these quotes were taken have been declassified and can be read at <www.wanttoknow.info/010501operationnorthwoods>

CHAPTER FOUR

Conspiracy theories

Talk to the Annual Conference of the Liberation Alliance, London, 2002.

Before I begin, let me say that throughout this talk I use the terms Left and Right and far Left and far Right. I appreciate that they are inadequate but they are a convenient shorthand, I use them conventionally and I hope you will bear with me in this.

I am flattered, and not a little surprised to be here in this distinguished company. Looking at the rest of the programme, I have half a suspicion that I am here to provide some light relief.

I'm here at the invitation of Chris Tame.[1] In 1983, I co-founded a little magazine called *Lobster*. My co-founder and I were interested in what Peter Dale Scott had called parapolitics – spookery, the covert world – and we vaguely thought maybe it could be written about in the UK, as it was being done in the United States. Chris Tame was then involved in the Alternative Bookshop, in Covent Garden, and somehow – I've forgotten how – he began selling this little magazine I produced. Once he mentioned my magazine in the Libertarian Alliance's magazine, *Free Life*, and described me as a libertarian socialist. Which was amusing: I am neither a proper libertarian nor a proper socialist. The nearest I got to being a socialist is joining the Labour Party; and the nearest I got to being a libertarian was when I was 16 and 17, hanging about with a group of beatniks in the mid 1960s, who laughingly called themselves the Edinburgh Anarchists. I can remember trying to read a book by Bakunin called, I seem to remember, *Scientific Anarchism* or *Science and Anarchism*. I couldn't understand it but it felt pretty cool – hip, as we used to say then – to be carrying it about.

What I – what the magazine *Lobster* – had that was of value to Tame was an interest in the activities of the British and American secret states. In a tiny way, *Lobster* was the enemy of the British state; as, in a more substantial way, was Chris Tame. On the basis that my enemy's enemy is my friend – the only meaningful dictum in politics – *Lobster* was embraced by Tame. Our interest in the nefarious doings of our secret servants and secret servants in general, extended to an interest in the conspiracy theories of the period. But not just any conspiracy theories: about French, German, Dutch or New Zealand conspiracy theories I know almost nothing. The conspiracy theories we were interested in were those coming out of the United States.

The problem I have is with the term 'conspiracy theory'. It means different things to different people. With the International Jewish Conspiracy theory, the *Protocols of the Elders of Zion nonsense*, as an exemplar, conspiracy theory began by referring to attempts to explain big geopolitical events by the imputed actions of hidden forces or groups: international Jewry; or Jewish bankers; the Catholic Church, the Masons and the Communist Party of the former Soviet Union have been the most popular candidates in Western Europe and America. Conspiracy theory's first general use was in the phrase 'the conspiracy theory of history'; and in the 20th century this originally referred to a cluster of ideas found on the authoritarian or fascist Right; and often was a code for 'the Jewish conspiracy theory'.

Almost everyone is keen to disassociate themselves from 'the conspiracy theory of history'. In academic, political and media circles, said of something, 'That's just a conspiracy theory', is often enough to condemn it, unconsidered, into the outer darkness – hopeless, beyond the pale. In dismissing something as 'just a conspiracy theory', or someone as a 'conspiracy theorist', the connotations of the oldest use of conspiracy theory – the irrational beliefs, the absence of evidence, or the misuse of evidence – are attributed and the subject or author is thus contaminated with them.

How often have you heard someone – an academic, a journalist perhaps – begin a sentence with 'Of course while I don't believe in'; or 'While I'm not a subscriber to the conspiracy theory of history . . .' and then, having inoculated themselves against the possibility of this heinous charge, they describe this or that particular conspiracy. This is reminiscent of the formula, 'Of course I'm not an anti-semite', followed by some anti-Jewish remark. I met a Tory businessman. He got half-cut at lunch and leaned over the table towards me and said,

'I'm not an anti-Semite but have you ever wondered why there are so many Jews in Mrs Thatcher's cabinet?' I hadn't, as it happens. And yes, when he listed them, they constituted a fifth of her cabinet at one time. It was positively *nostalgic* to hear the good old Jewish conspiracy theory emanating from a crusty, old, right-wing Tory with bad breath.

There is something strikingly, almost uniquely, dangerous about the word 'conspiracy' for Anglo-American intellectuals. Given its earlier associations with the authoritarian or anti-semitic right – at root the danger of being linked with Hitler – this isn't terribly surprising in a sense. But as much political, economic, intelligence and military activity is manifestly, structurally, and sometimes arguably, *properly* conspiratorial, this is a problem for people for whom the prohibition on conspiracy *theories* and the horror at being called a conspiracy *theorist* is absolute. The fear of conspiracy theories has extended to conspiracies *per se*. A case could be made – I won't try to make it here – that because of the conspiracy theory of history's connotations, conspiracy is the missing concept in the orthodox political and historical vocabulary.

Let me digress a little here. The title of this talk, 'In Defence of Paranoia', was suggested by Chris Tame and is a nod back to an essay I wrote in 1981 called 'In Defence of Paranoia Again'; and that title was a reference to an essay written during the early days of the Watergate affair, by Carl Oglesby, called, 'In Defence of Paranoia'. Carl Oglesby, an academic at MIT last time I saw him referred to, had been a student activist in the mid 1960s in SDS, Students for a Democratic Society. SDS agreed about opposing the war in Vietnam but not about much else and was riven by disputes between a variety of left groups – old CP, new CP and Trots. Trots or commies, new Left or old, it didn't matter: none of them paid any attention to the fact that between 1963 and 1968 both Robert and John Kennedy and Martin Luther King were assassinated by conspiracies which, when Oglesby wrote his essay, had not been seriously investigated officially; and still haven't been seriously investigated officially. The Kennedys and King were murdered by *successful* assassination conspiracies.

Unlike his peers, Oglesby had noticed the assassinations. And they were rather significant: the American liberal-left's three most important public figures were murdered, in public; and the murderers had been allowed to get away with it. The three 'assassins' were framed. Oswald – the 'evidence' against him was a crude joke. King's accused, James Earl Ray, confessed: he was given the choice, confess for a life sentence or they go for the death penalty. The evidence against him was never tested. The murder of Robert Kennedy by Sirhan Sirhan was collapsed by the autopsy evidence: RFK was killed by a point-blank shot behind his left ear, at a range of two inches or less. Powder burns are unmistakable. Sirhan Sirhan was in front of him. This is utterly banal, by the way, once you read the literature; and when you see that, you see the scale of the deception that has been run by those defending the official, 'no conspiracy' version of these events.

If we are going to think about the nature of American politics these events seem absolutely central to me. To use a wonderful Americanism I heard recently, the assassinations are the turd in the punchbowl. And this is how they seemed to Oglesby in 1973. Never mind what the text books tell us American political life is *supposed* to be like, let's start with the big stuff, the public assassination of leading figures. Of course, no-one does. Respectable political and academic America is united in almost nothing but there is virtual unanimity that all such talk as mine is irrational, probably an expression of some psychological defect – paranoia, usually – the sign of an intellectual cretin and, possibly, the sign of a closet racist.

Academic American history and American politics – and American politicians – continue to simply ignore, to *flunk* these events. Historians of contemporary America have given themselves a dispensation: we need not bother with this; we can just nod as we skirt it, accepting the official versions. I cannot think of a single American academic historian who is interested in these assassinations. The handful of academics with such an interest are all in other fields.

This began as a digression and it does get back to where I started, for the assassination of JFK in 1963 was the moment when the meaning of the term 'conspiracy theory' began to change from being something associated solely with a minority on the far Right of politics. After a chunk of JFK's skull bounced onto the boot of his car, 'conspiracy theory' ceased solely to evoke grandiose attempts to explain the history of a country or the world, by the actions of some hidden cabal.

Anthony Summers is one of our best, and one of our best paid investigative writers, who has written books on JFK's death, the Profumo Affair and J. Edgar Hoover. He was asked once to respond to the charge that he was a conspiracy theorist. He replied: 'I am not interested in conspiracy theories. But I am interested in theories about conspiracies.' JFK's assassination is the beginning of that shift from conspiracy theories to theories about conspiracies.

After JFK, to the discourse of mostly ridiculous tales from the Right about secret cabals, was added tales of real political conspiracies, many of them the work of the secret organs of the state, the CIA, the KGB, MI5 and so on. The new allegations of conspiracy were more modest in scale: they did not try to explain the decline of Christian America, say, or the fall of the British Empire – but this death, that coup, or this smear story. After JFK, and partly as the result of research by 'kooks and cranks' researching the Kennedy assassination, the secret states in the Western democracies begin to be revealed.

Following JFK's death in 1963, we have the King and Bobby Kennedy assassinations, the murder of much of the leadership of the Black Panthers; we have the collection of scandals known as Watergate; and, following that, in 1974-76, a period of inquiry and revelation as the world discovered some of what the CIA and FBI had been doing in America and abroad: bugging, tapping, smearing, plotting coups and assassinations; experimenting on unwitting people, including LSD and other forms of 'mind control'; and routinely interfering in the politics of many foreign countries – in short, doing rather similar things to those being done by the Soviet bloc at the time.

Looking at the growing catalogue of covert operations by US government agencies against *Americans*, Carl Oglesby suggested that conspiracy is normal politics carried out by normal means. Abbie Hoffman declared that conspiracy is American as apple pie. The political journalist, Ralph J. Gleason, formulated his First Law of Politics after Watergate: no matter how paranoid you are what they're doing is worse than you could possibly imagine. This was nicely illustrated shortly after when we learned that, as part of its experiments with drugs in the 1950s, the CIA had created a phoney brothel in which the unsuspecting customers were given LSD and secretly filmed. National Security can be a wonderful thing sometimes; it allows all manner of projects to be undertaken. There are people who think the entire drug culture in America and the West was a CIA project which got out of control. Lovely idea, for which there is, alas, no evidence.

Skimming the headlines of major conspiratorial scandals in America, after the CIA/FBI/Cold War revelations of the mid 1970s we continue into:

- Koreagate – the Korean CIA were bribing US politicians, with US money, to keep the US in South Korea.

- The October Surprise – the Republicans did a deal with the Iranian militants holding US hostages in Iran that they would keep them 'til after the 1980 American election, so damaging the Democrats.
- Iran-Contra – Congress cut off funds for the war against Nicaragua so Oliver North and his chums sold weapons to Iran to raise money for the Contras.
- The great cocaine scandal in which the CIA received permission from the Attorney General to turn a blind eye to cocaine imports into America, if the dealers gave money to the Contras.
- There are some people who look at the way the CIA has been allied to the drug traffic since the 1950s and wonder if the CIA isn't *running* the world's drug traffic. Another lovely idea, for which again there is, alas, no evidence.
- The Savings and Loan fraud in which billions of dollars were looted from America's savings banks; and so on and so on.

In the 1990s, things begin to shift. With the arrival of Bill Clinton and a Democrat government, the Republican Right began to generate conspiracy theories about the Clintons: Clinton a communist, Clinton a crook, Clinton a drug dealer, Clinton – or his circle – murdering witnesses by the truck load. A Clinton death list document circulating in 1998 listed forty deaths said to be suspicious among people who knew or were connected to Bill Clinton.

The one allegation the Republican Right showed no interest in was that made by Richard Goodwin, a

Kennedy adviser, who was told by a CIA source that the young Bill Clinton had been recruited by the CIA to keep tabs on other young American students in the UK while he was on his Rhodes scholarship at Oxford. This was the CIA's Operation Chaos, monitoring anti-war movements. Would an ambitious young Bill Clinton turn down the chance to help his country?

In the midst of this vast explosion of knowledge on America's secret or suppressed history, the traditional left-right divide began to blur a little. In the 1970s it was people on the American Left who began looking at the policy groupings of American and American-dominated capital: the Council on Foreign Relations and transnational groups like the Trilateral Commission and Bilderberg group. The best book I know on the Council on Foreign Relations was published by that most venerable of American Marxist journals, *The Monthly Review*. There is a well known book edited by Holly Sklar, *Trilateralism*, published in 1980. In the early 1980s people like me bought it. For the last decade it has almost exclusively been bought by the Right, by what we might call the New World Order theorists, who range from pretty serious researchers of the Council on Foreign Relations etc, to the people who believe the UN is on the verge of taking over the United States and warn their readers to Watch out for those UN troops in their blue berets!

You get a hint of how this overlapping of left and right happened from the subtitle of Sklar's book: *The Trilateral Commission and Elite Planning for World Management. Elite planning* . . . Though I don't suppose Sklar intended it, 'elite' was a key term among the conspiracy theorists of the Right. They might not all agree on which elite was secretly running the Fed, debauching the currency, running America into the ground and preparing to hand it over to the New World Order, but they were all agreed it was an *elite*. Not the people.

In the 1960s, it was the radical Left who began writing of Amerika, with a K instead of the C. In the 1990s, it was a section of the radical Christian Right which claimed to see an American Reich being created by the Clinton administration and the federal government; and some of them began to spell America with a K. And what happened? The Feds confirmed their worst imaginings at Ruby Ridge and Waco, Texas, treating a family in the backwoods and a fringe Christian group as if they were terrorists and killing over 80 of them. Cue the American militia movement.

As the Right in the 1980s and 90s embraced items from what had been a left agenda, some on the American Left took fright and began to distance themselves from the Right – and any talk of conspiracy. There is almost nothing the Left fears more than being associated in some way with the Right. We are dealing with concepts and psychological forces here such as purity and contamination. The major media noticed this apparent crossover and it was described as fusion paranoia . . . Of course the degree of fusion was slight, in fact, but the description was a splendid piece of psywar, bundling Left and Right together and labelling them both as 'paranoid'.

Why the explosion of interest in conspiracy theories in the 1990s? Partly it has been technology: computers, faxes and most important of all, the Internet. When Chris Tame and I were poking around in this stuff in the early 1980s, we were handling book and magazines – often expensive and often hard to find. Now almost anyone can broadcast to the world via the net or produce their own magazine. But the conspiracy boom has also partly been a creation of the US state. For the fingerprints of the US state are visible on the explosion of theories which appeared in the 1990s around the subject of UFOs. A multi-agency group of US scientists and spooks began a series of disinformation projects around UFOs in the 1980s. The content of the disinformation project was aliens, abductions by aliens, landings, crashed alien vehicles and secret activity in the 1950s in these fields by the US government. Documents were fabricated then 'leaked'; other documents were fabricated and planted in the national archives as backstops, to be 'found'. These confirmed the earlier, leaked documents, as genuine. If this all sounds familiar it may be because much of this turned up in The X Files, the most successful American TV series of the 1990s which, in turn, produced other TV spin-offs, series, documentaries, movies and a whole shelf of magazines. When The X Files broke big, the people who created these disinformation projects must have broken out their best cigars, those big illegal Cuban cigars. What a coup! The highest compliment that could be paid to a disinformation project in peacetime: the themes you invented had become prime time, No. 1 in the ratings.

Why this was done – we don't know. Some of the available information suggests that the project began with the specific aim of disinforming one man, one UFO buff who had recorded evidence of something odd going on at an American Air Force base. This man, not very stable to begin with, was fed a pile of hogwash about aliens by US Air Force personnel; and he then broadcast the news that the US Air Force had told him about aliens to the UFO buff community, where it spread like wild-fire. At which point the people in charge of disinforming this one individual seem to have decided to do something bigger with the stories they had created. Here all manner of speculations arise. Did they use it to see what they could persuade people to believe? A psy-war experiment? Creating a new threat to replace the fading Cold War? Were they just exploring the gullibility of UFO buffs? Was it simply another use of the UFO theme to provide cover stories for experimental US planes? For the CIA has admitted it used the UFO story as a way of concealing the U2 programme in the 1950s. I don't know; and so far they haven't said.

The vast compendium of these UFO tales, The X Files, produced a spin-off programme called Dark Skies. The writers of Dark Skies took one of the most preposterous of the themes in the UFO cannon, the idea that some kind of deal had been done in the 1950s between the extraterrestrial aliens and the US government, and presented a new version of post-war American history in which aliens featured at the key points – Dealey Plaza, Watergate and so on. The programme and its title, Dark

Skies, is an apt symbol for the change in white American society since the early 1950s. In the 50s, white Americans whistled along to Blues Skies – 'Only blue skies from now on'. I haven't checked but in my memory Doris Day is singing it. 40 years of the National Security State at home and the prosecution of the American empire abroad, and we have Dark Skies and the alien take-over of the United States presented in literal form: not the Red Menace, nor the John Birch Society's insiders, or, its later equivalent, the New World Order of the 1990s, but literal alien spacemen. Aliens had ceased to be foreigners or foreign ideologies and had become . . . aliens.

Why this has happened sociologically – the under-lying cause – I think is the decline in the standard of living of the (white) American citizen as the so-called 'free market' in America redistributes from middle to top. Most Americans have no access to, nor have been accustomed to using, the kind of concepts with which to explain their declining standard of living and the chaos in their inner cities. What they do have access to and can handle is a kind of nativist, conspiratorial discourse – if I can use that word without evoking the dreaded post-modernists – in which the question that is asked is not What is the explanation for this? But: Who is responsible for this? Who is *behind* this? It remains to be seen if the experience in the last couple of years with Enron and the rest of it, the discovery that the banking and investment system appears to be designed to steal their savings, begins to shift the focus of attention onto structural questions. In my casual browsing through the conversations of the American populist Right on these issues there seem to be faint signs of a light dawning that all may not be well with the American social and economic system.

If there hasn't really been a fusion of left-right paranoia, there has appeared a kind of almost apolitical conspiracy culture in which all appearances are false, everything is a conspiracy. One of the better magazines which has carried this material, has the slogan on its front cover: All Conspiracy, No Theory. In this conspiracy culture there are no normal political processes; politicians never act for reasons other than greed, self-interest, because they're being blackmailed by somebody, or because they are somebody's agent; and there are no accidents or coincidences. Into this conspiracy cyber-culture the events of the eleventh of September, 9/11, detonated like a hurricane.

Two weeks ago I asked the Google search engine to look for '9/11, conspiracy' and got 83,000 hits. 83,000! Most of those, I'm sure, are arguing that there was a conspiracy of some kind of other; that it wasn't what it looked like; that it was a fake. Either that the planes were being flown by remote control, or that the al-Qaeda pilots were stooges for the CIA or Mossad; or that it was allowed to happen. For what it's worth, my view at present is that both elements of conspiracy and cock-up are involved here. On the conspiracy side, I think some sections of the sprawling, squabbling US intelligence community knew something was coming down the pipeline from al-Qaeda, and decided to let it happen. An attack on Afghanistan was being planned anyway and a terrorist incident would provide a convenient *causus beli* and enable a whole bunch of repressive legislation which was already drafted to be run through a Congress paralysed by the fear of being thought unpatriotic. The evidence of advance but not quite-specific warnings, by the bucket-load, is now undeniable; and the speculation just before the incident in the shares of airlines is suggestive. The cock-up side is that the 'incident' turned out to be much bigger than they imagined. Some of the relatives of the dead have begun a class action lawsuit against the US government for, as they put it, letting it happen on purpose. This one is going to run and run, especially now that the ambulance-chasers have it in their sights.[2]

It comes down to the question of what the world is like, what is going on? And in this contest over the nature of political reality, the term conspiracy theory these days has two uses. The major media use it as a way of kicking stories off the news agenda. If you want journalists to hang up the phone, use the word conspiracy in your opening sentences. No matter what else you say and no matter how cogently and rationally you present the information, you will have triggered the journalist's 'I'm dealing with a nutter' programme, a kind of firewall in the brain which prevents the dreaded virus of conspiracy infecting them.

The orthodox political centre uses it to screen out ideas which might disturb it. Political orthodoxy, which we might call pluralism, tells us that there are many political or interest groups in society all of whom seek power. In the pluralist model there is little room for, to take just two examples, corrupt politicians and covert operations by secret servants of the state. Robert Caro's third volume on the career of Lyndon Baines Johnson, *Master of the Senate*, is another massive piece of research full of wonderful bits and pieces. But the one thing Caro doesn't try to explain in the 1000 pages on Johnson's career in the 1950s, is how Johnson got to be so rich. He doesn't quite avoid it but while Caro gives us dozens of pages on relatively minor incidents in the Senate, on Johnson's obnoxious personality and strange personal habits, he is strikingly incurious about how LBJ made his money. It's not that how LBJ made his money is a secret: he took bribes, of course. That's partly how American politics works: money talks and bullshit walks, to quote one of the congressman filmed by the FBI during the Abscam investigations of the 1980s. It's just that we don't have many details on LBJ's corruption and I vaguely hoped that Caro would provide them. It will be interesting to see how Caro handles the events in the 1960-63 period of Johnson's career in his next volume. For in those years, LBJ became enmired in domestic scandal, events, which we have learned recently, climaxed with LBJ's little criminal gang in Texas murdering President Kennedy.

And since Kennedy's assassination marks the beginning of the current conspiracy theory culture, it is an appropriate place to stop and take contributions from the floor.

Notes

1 Chris Tame died in 2006. In *Lobster* 51 I wrote this:

'Chris Tame, founder of the Libertarian Alliance, died of cancer in March. He was 55. An obituary by his friend Sean Gabb is at <www.seangabb.co.uk/flcomm/flc 144.htm>.

Tame was a very intelligent and amusing man with an enormous blind spot. Like many on the radical left, Tame, on the radical right, believed that people were just itching to be set free to take control of their own lives. Unfortunately, many – perhaps most – people don't want to take charge of their lives. Where those on the left with the delusion about people's urge to be independent turned to Marxism-Lenisim, syndicalism, trade union activism etc. as the best means of achieving the people's liberation, Chris turned to classical liberal economics and the notion of what we might call property-owning anarchism as the means to that end.

After Mrs Thatcher left office we had a long telephone conversation in which Tame expressed his disillusionment with Thatcher and many of her works. He – and, I presume, others with his views – really had believed when she took office in 1979 that the libertarian dawn was upon them. 'L'actualité' was a profound disappointment. As I listened to him, it struck me that in relation to the reality of Thatcherism, he was in a directly analogous position to those socialists in the Labour Party who thought the Labour governments of the sixties heralded a socialist Britain and never forgave Wilson and Labour for the 'betrayal'.

2. Several class action suits were begun, of which one, aimed at Al Qaeda, appears to be still active.

CHAPTER FIVE

The Kennedy Assassination

A talk given in Liverpool in 1995 to Dallas 63, a group of people interested in the Kennedy assassination.

When the idea of talking here tonight was first put to me, my reaction was 'What can I tell them? They probably know more than I do.' I am by no means a serious JFK buff. That subject is one of many that I attempt to keep some track of. I haven't even read all the books on the case, let alone done any more detailed research. When I reach forensic or acoustic material in the books, I skip them. I have no specialised area. My interest in the case is general – and political. The Kennedy assassination was the lens through which I, along with many other people, first began to study American politics.

For the assassination said: this is a society – a political system – in which the President was shot in broad daylight and the body politic – his professional colleagues – did not feel able to look for the truth. This is a very striking and radicalising fact; which is why, I guess, so much time and effort has gone into trying to maintain the cover-up.

It is possible to get pessimistic about the case, and conclude that while the amount of material appearing appears to increase – what with FBI releases and FOIA requests and so forth – we are in fact getting no closer to anything resembling a solution. I actually don't think this. It seems to me that though we don't know who ordered the assassination, or, indeed, who pulled the trigger; or, even, that a shot was fired from the Grassy Knoll by a man wearing a Dallas Police uniform, as that computer enhanced photograph seemed to suggest, we actually know – or can reasonably infer – a good deal about the case now. It sometimes seems to me that the case suffers now from too much investigation and too little thinking. Tonight I offer you a little general thinking, and I'll do it by reference to my own thinking since I got interested in the case in 1976.

I came to the assassination via a US conspiracy theory called the Skeleton Key to the Gemstone File which was imported and circulated here by a couple of London anarchists. Intrigued, I read some of the books that were then available – surprisingly few, looking back on it. Then I found out about Harry Irwin and he began bunging stuff my way: the Torbitt Memorandum and Sprague and *Farewell America*, I remember. To my amazement, I discovered that Hull University had the entire 26 Warren Commission volumes – which no-one, before me, had ever borrowed, incidentally – and I even skimmed my way through them. Initially I couldn't get past the Cui bono? Who benefits? question. Who gained from JFK's death? But as my knowledge increased, it became clear that Who benefits? tells us nothing because it tells us too much. There were simply too many candidates. The Mafia, the military, the intelligence agencies,

Vice President Johnson, sundry American politicians on the verge of public disgrace – notably Johnson's protégé Bobby Baker – the FBI, the oil companies, the far Right, various Latin American dictators, the Vietnam war lobby, even the Italian Right threatened by Kennedy's willingness to tolerate the Italian socialists – all of them benefited from the death of Kennedy. Following Cui bono?, you ended up in a situation a bit like the version of the killing in the first volume of the *Illuminatus Trilogy* by Shea and Wilson, in which several teams of assassins, representing different organisations, find themselves bumping into each other on the grassy knoll, all trying to get a shot off at the presidential limousine.

The second big development for me was realising that you had to separate the assassination from the cover-up. After Who benefits?, like many others, I was hypnotised by the cover-up. From the cover-up, we thought, you could read backwards and find out who organised the shooting. But it became clear, as the links between Oswald and various bureaucracies were revealed – the FBI and the CIA in particular – that these bureaucracies had reasons to cover things up *whether or not* they had been involved in the shooting. Oswald's name popping up in the files of the CIA, FBI – and possibly Naval Intelligence; and God knows who else – was the shit hitting the fan; and we now know that bureaucracies, and especially those kinds of bureaucracies, faced with embarrassment go into cover-up mode automatically.

The FBI were embarrassed at several levels: they hadn't kept an eye on Oswald and were afraid they would be blamed for the assassination. Hoover, in particular, was then under considerable pressure to resign and make way for a younger, less communist-obsessed man. Irony of ironies, here was a presidential assassination apparently carried out by that rarest of rarities, an American Marxist defector to the Soviet Union – and right under the noses of the great red hunters, the FBI. It is also extremely likely that the FBI had been using Oswald as part of their Cointelpro operations against the Fair Play for Cuba Committee, though Freedom of Information requests have failed to turn up a single significant page on the FBI's Cointelpro operations against the Fair Play for Cuba Committee. Oswald, we may assume, was working as a low-level informant for the FBI, and as an agent provocateur, tasked to set up a phoney Fair Play for Cuba Committee, a honey-trap for the local Left. His curious behaviour in New Orleans, all that activity with the anti-Castro Cubans; his radio talk, his arrest for giving out hands-off Cuba leaflets; his contacting of the various American left groups; his work with the Guy Bannister agency – it is all most consistent with Oswald creating an identity for himself as a lefty, pro-Castro activist, while working for the FBI, probably at arms-length, through Bannister. There is quite a lot of evidence now on the FBI's use of former agents, such as Bannister, in such deniable operations.

The CIA had just as much to conceal about his links with them. His false defection, just for starters, which was probably – but not yet certainly, to my knowledge – a CIA operation. Then his links with De Morenschild and the other white Russians in the Dallas area amongst whom Oswald was deposited on his return from the Soviet Union. This whole episode is very odd indeed. Where does the Marxist former defector go? To a group of wealthy white – anti-Soviet – Russian expatriots in the far Right's major stronghold, Dallas. De Morenschild, who seems to have been baby-sitting Oswald in this period, called those white Russians in Dallas, 'Solidarists'. It's in his testimony to the Warren Commission. And what are Solidarists? Members or supporters of NTS, an anti-Soviet group which had been run since the end of the Second World War first by the British SIS and then, after 1956, by the CIA. Put it this way: if you had to define a group who would be *least* likely to adopt a Marxist former defector, it might be an anti-Soviet group, run by the CIA, in Dallas. Oswald was met on his arrival in the US by a man from a CIA front group, and was resettled among personnel of a CIA operation.

Then there was the Agency's war against Cuba, still officially secret in 1963, despite the massive operation in the southern coastal states. Oswald's connections with the anti-Castro Cubans threatened to reveal some of that.

So: Oswald had intelligence fingerprints all over him, and it isn't hard to imagine the flap in the CIA and FBI on 22/11/63. Now that we know how these agencies behave – and it is worth remembering that in 1963 the public knew almost nothing of this – in retrospect it is blindingly obvious that the one thing all the intelligence bureaucracies would do is hit the shredders and start putting out disinformation about Oswald and their links with him.

The evidence is reasonably clear that in the immediate aftermath of the shooting, a small group on the fringe of the intelligence services tried to use Oswald's false pro-Castro identity to blame the assassination on Cuba (or the Soviet Union), presumably in the hope of pushing the US government into adopting a more anti-Cuban stance, and perhaps engineering an invasion of the island. But official Washington, still recovering from the shock of the Cuban missile crisis the year before, had to block this line of speculation. Hence the vehement assertion 24 hours after the event of the 'lone assassin' verdict. All the American agencies of state in the immediate aftermath of the shooting had a vested interest in a 'no conspiracy' verdict, *whether they believed it or not.* 'No conspiracy' was the only safe option; it cuts off all possible inquiries. We are talking about politics here; and in politics the truth is never the primary consideration.

It is this, I suggest, which explains the extraordinary business which David Lifton so convincingly investigated in his *Best Evidence*. Lifton's book is a wonderful piece of research in which he proves that the corpse was altered to make the wounds fit the 'lone assassin', 'no conspiracy', decision. Lifton shows this beyond a reasonable doubt, in my view.[1] But what does this mean? Lifton seems to end up arguing that altering of the corpse was part of the original plan. This then means that the original plan was massive, involving all kinds of high-level military personnel. But hang on a minute; this is an absurdity. Lifton wants us to believe that a group of senior military personnel would adopt a plan which relied (a) on getting uninterrupted access to the body after the event, and (b) on the corpse being in a sufficiently intact condition to be convincingly reconstructed. What if Kennedy's entourage had refused to give up possession? What if the Dallas authorities had insisted on their jurisdiction over the corpse? What if the shooting had been more accurate and Kennedy's head had been hit by several shots and had been too badly damaged? I don't think the US military are very good or very bright, on the whole, but I find it inconceivable that a group of senior US military would give the go-ahead for a plan which hinged on so many variables potentially beyond their control. To my knowledge Lifton has never responded to this most obvious objection.

After 30 years of watching US intelligence and military bureaucracies routinely cover-up everything, from Dallas, through Watergate, through Iran-Contra and the other intelligence scandals of the Reagan-Bush era, we simply have to acknowledge that the fact that they covered-up after Oswald's arrest, alas, *tells us nothing in particular*. The investigation of the cover-up has been enormously informative about the behaviour of the US intelligence bureaucracies, and their links with the media, but it tells us nothing about the conspiracy. We are, as it were, thrown back onto the event itself.

There are four shootings in the case; Kennedy, Oswald, Tippit and Governor Connally. The Tippit murder seems to me to be a red herring; just a coincidence. Oswald patently didn't do it and I have seen nothing which substantially links his death to the other shootings that day. So I propose to remove him from the picture. If we were going to be tough-minded about this we might argue that no-one has yet *proved* that the *intended* target was JFK. Connally was hit by at least as many shots as Kennedy and might have been the target. I have a vague memory of a witness – Jarnigan? I haven't looked this up for a long time – who claimed to have heard Oswald and Ruby talking about assassinating Connally; and there are rumours that Connally, as Governor of Texas, was in the way of some kind of mob expansion into Texas. So this is a possibility, still, I guess. However, without more substantial evidence on this we may as well accept the general view that Kennedy was the target and Connally was just in the wrong place at the wrong time.

But the original plan was not just to assassinate the president, but to assassinate the president *and* frame Lee Harvey Oswald: the murder plus its solution; a nice, neat package. And the plan must have been to leave a *dead*, framed assassin. This was essential; for a live patsy, especially one as intelligent as Oswald, was a liability. Alive he would have talked – did talk, though what he said has been suppressed. So, the original plan was shoot Kennedy, leave a dead, incriminated patsy. And like so many plans, it went wrong. Oswald didn't die immediately after the shooting. My guess is that the plan was that he would die resisting arrest – a fairly routine occurrence where American police forces are concerned. Whatever his actual role, Oswald appears to have made an arrangement to meet someone in that cinema that afternoon. By all accounts cinemas were a popular rendezvous for intelligence agents. In the cinema, when the police grabbed him, a gun misfired – allegedly Oswald's, but more likely a policeman's in my view. And Oswald shouted, 'I am not resisting arrest, I am not resisting arrest'. That piece of quick-witted thinking on Oswald's part probably saved his life. For the police could then not risk shooting him; there were too many witnesses in the cinema. This, of course, suggests that the Dallas Police – or some of them – were in on the conspiracy. This was General De Gaulle's view: the police had to be in on it; and De Gaulle knew something about assassination attempts.

But with Oswald in custody, a live patsy, the conspiracy had a major problem. Oswald had to die before he came to court.

Because the patsy was supposed to be dead, the frame-up didn't have to be very good. And it wasn't. Had it come to trial any half-decent lawyer would have reduced the frame to tatters. There was no decent evidence linking LHO to the event. No ballistics evidence – a dud rifle, to start with. No eyewitnesses linking him with the shooting. The people working with Oswald in the Book Depository would have been called as witnesses and shown that he could not have fired the shots and got back to the canteen where he was found. The 'second Oswald' activities would have come unstuck had Oswald come to trial and been proved to be elsewhere at the time he was seen shooting. The photographs showing Oswald posing with the rifle, which he claimed were faked, would have been examined. And so forth. It was crudely done – just enough to provide the set dressing for the dead president/dead assassin scenario. With a dead Oswald there would have been no need for a major inquiry; no Warren Commission would have been created. It would all have been done and dusted, a neat little package served up to the American public through the media. As it was, the Warren Commission had to labour long and hard, going through the motions of a real investigation to come up with the verdict desired by the political system.[2]

Many, though not all, of the early dissenting researchers in the US were more or less on the Left, and many, though not all, wanted to find the fingerprints of the American state on the event. But thirty years later, what have we found? Sadly, from my viewpoint on the anti-American British Left, nothing of substance. This is not terribly surprising in my view. Would agencies as powerful as the CIA or FBI have needed to do something as crude as bushwhack him in public? Could they not have found more subtle ways to kill him? I find it difficult to imagine that senior CIA, FBI or military personnel would ever have sanctioned a plan as risky as that of a public ambush, at long-range, on a moving target. It might well have failed – and almost did fail: there was only one killing shot, after all. And it wasn't as if they were short of examples of how difficult this was to do: there had been many failed attempts to knock off de Gaulle (some of which it is said the CIA had a hand in, though the evidence on this is thin). No, though some of the CIA and the military chiefs disliked Kennedy for his attempts to cool the Cold War with the Soviet Union, I find it deeply improbable that any of them would have sanctioned such a high-risk strategy as a public assassination – especially using a patsy who had traceable links back to the Agency, the FBI and the US military. Indeed, would they have needed to kill him at all? Could they not have simply revealed some of his sexual activities to the American public and discredited him?

Which brings me to the third important recognition in my thinking about this case. The assassination in Dallas was a crude, high risk operation which went wrong: the designated patsy survived and had to be silenced, in public. Enter Jack Ruby. It took me nearly fifteen years of interest in the case to acknowledge that Ruby's role is strong evidence that the Mafia shot Kennedy. Like many others, I simply didn't want an event as dramatic as this, and with such far-reaching consequences, to have such a banal conclusion. But who steps forward to solve the conspirators' Oswald problem? The Mob's man in Dallas. If there is any evidence that Ruby had intelligence connections, I am not aware of them. He may have been a low level criminal informant for the FBI earlier in his career, but in Dallas his role seems unambiguous. Looking back on the years when I was fixated on the CIA, I am baffled as to how I managed to push Ruby's role to the back of my mind. Because Ruby is all over the event; reliably reported meeting Oswald before the assassination; at Parkland Hospital shortly after the arrival of the body; at a press conference, correcting an error by District Attorney Wade in the attribution of

Oswald's Cuban links. You could make a reasonable, if sketchy case for Ruby having a substantial role in the assassination as a kind of manager, tidying up loose ends, dotting 'i's and crossing 't's.

The case for the Mafia as the culprits is very strong. They had the means; killing people is something they did routinely. Killing a president is something a bit special, but it is clear from the many intercept transcripts of Mafia personnel talking that the mob did not hold the President in awe. He was just Joe Kennedy's son, Frank Sinatra's friend, another shyster politician, who had welshed on deals they thought had been done. It is now clear that the Mob fixed the 1960 election for Kennedy. The Mob had the motive – they were being seriously hassled by the Justice Department headed by Robert Kennedy. We know, again from FBI intercepts, that they talked repeatedly of killing both Kennedys. The event itself, the crudity of the method chosen – bushwhacking him in public – the role of Ruby clearing up the mess, and the fact that people in or close to the Mob, right down to minor figures like Rose Cheramie, knew about the assassination in advance – all of this says the Mafia did it.

The major argument against the Mafia-did-it thesis has always been that powerful though they might have been, they did not have the power to organise the cover-up which followed the event. But that argument only has force if you *assume* that the crime and the cover-up were the work of the same people; and, as I tried to show earlier, this is neither necessary nor even sensible.

I don't like the idea that the Mob did it. I'd much rather it was a conspiracy by the spooks or the military. But there it is. Jack Ruby's role *alone* always said the Mob did it. And the Mob probably killed RFK, as well; afraid that, if elected, he would continue his war against them – and investigate their killing of his brother.

This all seems obvious, even banal to me now. But the Kennedy assassination has always been a kind of mirror which reflects the viewer's own preoccupations. So, as the intelligence services and their activities came to dominate American politics in the decade following Kennedy's death, it was them – and the war in Vietnam – which fascinated the better researchers.

And if you ask 'Well, if they're innocent of the murder, why do the US intelligence and security services continue to play cover-up games?', the answer lies in the consequences of a political cover-up. For once you have made the initial cover-up moves, you have to then cover-up the cover-up – and so on *ad infinitum*. Gerald Posner will not be last to try and squeeze this enormous rabbit back into the hat from whence it came.

Notes

1 I no longer believe this; and, frankly, I am faintly embarassed that I gave the thesis so much credence. I cannot remember why I did. More recent research suggests that there were two autopsies on men with gunshot wounds to the head that day in Dallas, the second one being done on Dallas policeman Tippit. Tippit looked very similar to JFK and received similar wounds. It may be that the autopsies done on the two men were switched or muddled, presumably the former. Search for 'JFK autopsy' pictures on Google Images and you will see the two sets of pictures. In some, JFK is presented with the back of his head a mass of blood and brains. In others he is presented with the back of his head intact.

They can't be the same head and the pictures showing an intact rear of the skull may be of Tippit.

2 Some believe there were two 'Oswalds'. See next chapter, especially Note 1.

Comments

I no longer think the Mob did it. Evidence which has appeared since this talk in 1995 makes it pretty clear, but not absolutely certain, that JFK was killed by people around his Vice President, Lyndon Johnson. This is discussed in my book on the case *Who Shot JFK?* (Pocket Essentials, 2007) I was right to suspect that the audience at Dallas 63 would know more than me. They did; and as soon as I finished my spiel they went off into their various specialities, leaving me far behind.

CHAPTER SIX

Traditions in Euro-American Conspiracy Theories: How competent are conspirators?

Talk given to the Fortean Times Unconvention, London, 1998.

Well, here we are again. I was at this august ceremony two years ago. I notice the attendance is down this year. Has the conspiracy bubble burst? Or has everyone gone to the other session to check out which of her stunning frocks Jenny Randles is wearing today?

I have a confession to make: I was seriously tempted to find the text of my talk of two years ago and simply read it again. Who would remember? I certainly don't remember what I said. But I didn't: this is a brand new bit of spiel. At any rate, I think it's new. But who knows? Maybe I've written the same thing again. There is a pretty limited range of things which can be said about this subject.

The title of this talk is 'How competent are conspirators?' The choice of title wasn't mine. It was suggested by a member of the John Brown Publishing staff who organise this event. I didn't like it much as a title and when it was suggested, I said I'd get back to him with a better one. But of course, I didn't. I couldn't *think* of a better one. Good titles are hard.

In the course of trying to elucidate what the Fortean wallahs wanted me to talk about – after all, conspiracy theories are pretty tangential to the *Fortean Times'* central interests – the John Brown staffer came up with this:

> *'In taking an overview of 'conspiracy theory lore', one could argue that there is a dichotomy between the intricacy of a conspiracy plan, and the way that the details of these plans tend to leak out to the general public. "If these conspirators are so clever, how come the crucial piece of evidence ends up being uncovered by an ordinary Joe", might be the starting point.'*

So, I'll start with that.

Alas, there is really no such beast as 'conspiracy theory lore'. I can understand why a Fortean alumnus would want there to be such a creature. Conspiracy theory lore would fit in nicely next to folk lore and UFO lore and give the subject that particular touch of the fascinating, the arcane and the fatuous which characterises the way the *Fortean Times* treats many of its subject areas. 'Lore', according to my Oxford pocket dictionary, is 'a body of traditions and facts on a subject'; and as far as conspiracy theory goes, there really isn't such a body of traditions and facts. There are really two broad traditions in Euro-American conspiracy theory.

The obvious starting point through this muddy field is the anti-semitic tradition, which produced the famous Czarist forgery, the *Protocols of the Elders of Zion*, a century or so ago, a document which survives today, chiefly in the Middle East, where it is endlessly reprinted and distributed by the enemies of Israel. But the Protocols were simply a particular spin on an established *tradition* of seeking to explain political change by the activities of secret groups of conspirators. That this view was common in the 19th century is hardly surprising. Most regimes were monarchies and most monarchies were run and policed by little groups of people round the King or Queen who faced constant opposition and plotting by rival groups. If Benjamin Disraeli thought that his contemporary Europe could be explained by the activities of little groups of secret conspirators – and it is a big if, supported only by a single quote from one of his novels, as far as I know – he was merely reporting his every day reality. The ruling elite of Britain in the late 19th century was very small: they knew each other, their children went to the same schools and universities and thence into the City, armed forces, the church or civil administration. Put like that, not a lot has changed, really, has it? Mr Blair's New Britain still looks like old, class-ridden Britain to me.

The anti-Jewish fantasies of the 19th century merged with the fear of Bolshevism in post World War 1 Europe and we get the Communism-is-Jewish variant which survives, in little pockets, on the far Right today. After WW2, in America, to the Jewish conspiracy theory and the communist conspiracy theory was added something which might best be described as a view of the conspiracy of the few, the elite, against the many; of anti-Americanisms of various hues against the purity and beauty of the true, native America. This took many forms. The least discussed is the anti-British version. During the early years of WW2, the British secret service created a massive intelligence and propaganda operation in the States which tried to discredit the isolationists and persuade the reluctant population to support US entry into the War. At the time, this was barely perceived by the US population – though J. Edgar Hoover had an idea of what was going on – and to this day, for pretty obvious reasons, has not really been taken seriously by Anglo-American academics. After the war this emerged in disguised form as the great anti-communist hysteria led by McCarthy and Hoover. But, look at the people that witch-hunt went after. For sure, some of them were communists or Soviet-sympathisers, but the witch-hunt began against members of the ramified network of US Anglophiles who had led the campaign in the early years of the war to get the US in.

This only became clear after the publication of Carroll Quigley's famous book *Tragedy and Hope* in 1966 which revealed the existence of the Round Table network, set up with Cecil Rhodes' money just before WW1. The discovery of this network, and especially the discovery of its US affiliates, notably the Council on Foreign Relations, shifted the focus, at any rate in the US, from whence most of this has come, away from communism, the Jewish conspiracy or an amalgam of both, onto this Anglophile elite.

The groups which most enthusiastically embraced this elite conspiracy, for example the John Birch Society, have their antecedents in the isolationist tendencies of the pre-WW2 era. The 1930s belief that the US ought not to get embroiled in the evil, decadent ways of Europe, has become today's populist hostility to the United Nations and the belief that the US elite is planning a New World Order in which the interests of ordinary Americans will be sacrificed to further the interests of what I recently saw described in a US newsletter as 'the Illuminati's Socialist/Communist/Freemasonic New World Order'. This illustrates nicely one of the characteristics of this strand of conspiracy theories: new theories don't supplant old ones, they're just added to them. The all-embracing description just quoted came from a David Smith in Waxahacie, Texas.

Insofar as we are aware of these various elite cabals, this is not due to some crucial piece of evidence being *discovered* by an ordinary Joe, as my Fortean correspondent put it. There never was a Jewish conspiracy, though there have been some conspiracies by Jews in the founding and maintenance of the state of Israel. The international communist conspiracy, real and imaginary, was in newspapers in every western society every week from 1920 to 1940. The Round Table network wasn't *discovered* by somebody poring over newspapers in the New York Public Library, like Mr Charles Forte, but was identified by one of its associates, 50 years after it was created, and 20 years after it had ceased to mean very much.

The ordinary Joe's role in all of this has been merely to consume and distort. It's not the *plans* of such groups which leak out, but the groups' *existence*. The Round

Table's views, from which some of their plans could be inferred, could be read in their journal, *The Round Table*, which is in many British universities. The Council on Foreign Relation's journal, *Foreign Affairs*, likewise. But first their *existence* had to become known. The Bilderberg Group, another gathering of the American-European elite, still tries very hard not to attract attention. But it has been regularly reported on in the USA in a magazine called *The Spotlight* for over a decade. One of its recent guests, a Tony Blair, has included his visit to a recent Bilderberg conference in his Parliamentary declaration of interests.

The latest in the long line of American-funded groups seeking to keep the British ruling elite pro-American is called the British American Project for the Successor Generation, or BAP for short. (I published a long article about them in *Lobster* 33.) You may not have heard about BAP because the major media in Britain have mostly ignored it, in the same way they mostly ignore Ditchley, the CFR, Bilderberg and the Trilateral Commission. But BAP runs a UK and US office and publishes a newsletter, albeit one to which you and I can't subscribe. In this, BAP members are kept up to date about the career developments of other BAP members. The BAP newsletter's message is clear enough: stick with us, boys and girls, and you'll go far. BAP, like the Round Table, the Council on Foreign Relations, Ditchley, Wilton Park, Chatham House *et al*, isn't so much a secret organisation, as a discreet organisation. This tradition of discreet, publicity-averse, elite gatherings will continue so long as the

British and American elites find them useful ways of agreeing an agenda and getting their views across without the impedance of the electorate and democracy. And, of course, such groupings will continue to be the subject of conspiracy-theorising, so long as they continue to look like conspiracies.

The second conspiracy theory tradition in the Anglo-American world concerns conspiracy theories about particular incidents in the violent world of American politics. Although there are lots of historical antecedents to the Kennedy assassination, it is those events in 1963 – and the killings of Robert Kennedy and Martin Luther King in 1968 – which really mark the beginning of this strand in conspiracy theory. The JFK incident has been the subject of over 800 books – of which I guess I've read about 60 – and it is now the subject of dozens of sites on the Net, and at least three serious journals. If you started now and devoted yourself full-time to getting up to speed on the literature, it would take several years. This is the big one, the Moby Dick of conspiracies. At the risk of boring you, especially the people here who know more about this than I do, I want to quickly browse through bits of it.

Let's go back, briefly, to the Warren Commission in 1964. The Warren Commission and its team of lawyers were specifically tasked *not* to investigate the shooting but to provide the evidence that Oswald, the 'lone nut', had done it. We now know that one of the chief preoccupations of those in charge in the White House, at the time, was preventing the assassination being used by anti-communist pressure groups within the US – the anti-Castro Cubans, notably – to trigger another invasion of Cuba by US forces. Within 24 hours of the shooting, the Deputy Attorney General, Katzenbach, had decided that the whole thing better be shut down. In the collective Washington memory, the Cuban Missile Crisis still loomed large. In such a climate, who really shot Kennedy was never an issue. As far as we can judge from the memoirs of those around at the time, nobody seems to have cared greatly. Kennedy's killer was of little consequence when measured against another nuclear showdown with the Soviet Union.

The federal government's major investigative body, the FBI, was happy that there was no serious investigation because they were in danger of being embarrassed at two levels. The first danger they faced was being exposed as grossly incompetent. If it was shown that Oswald, *qua* communist, had done the deed for political reasons, they had failed to prevent a 'communist' shooting the president. And Oswald had been a very public communist. He had been on TV as a communist, was corresponding with the Communist Party, the Socialist Workers Party, and the Fair Play for Cuba Committee – all of which were completely penetrated by the FBI. He had also defected to the Soviet Union and redefected; he was known to the FBI agent in Dallas. In the Cold War years in the United States, in the *southern* United States, Lee Harvey Oswald was about as public a communist as you could imagine. For the FBI to be exposed as not having prevented *him*, of all people, from shooting the president would have been a bureaucratic disaster. And there was the danger that Oswald would be revealed as an FBI informant, for which there is some evidence. So, the 'lone nut' verdict suited the FBI; and it suited the other American agencies, including the CIA, with whom Oswald had been involved in his curious career.

This was 1964; there was virtually no investigative journalism; large chunks of the US mass media had been co-opted by the CIA in the propaganda war with the Soviet Union. There was almost no autonomous American Left: most of it, we now know, was wholly or partly being run by the FBI. There was, in fact, virtually no critical community of any kind. Those who went through the motions of sitting on the Warren Commission assumed that they would produce the report, and the whole thing would be put to bed. One of the Commission members, former CIA chief Allen Dulles, famously said of the Report that it would only be read by a few professors. Since the whole thing was a charade, the evidence haphazardly accumulated by the Commission's team of lawyers, evidence - which included such fascinating titbits as a picture of Jack Ruby's mother's false teeth - was thrown together higgledy-piggledy in the famous 26 volumes, with no sense, no organisation and no index worth speaking of. It never occurred to those in charge that anyone would bother to look.

But they did. A number of ordinary US citizens bought one of the 1000 copies of the evidence which the government had printed and then began poring over it. One woman indexed the 26 volumes. Almost immediately the nature of the charade was revealed.

One individual who began studying the evidence was a graduate physics student at UCLA in California, David Lifton. His research begun in 1965, eventually produced the extraordinary book *Best Evidence* in 1980, which seems to show that the President's body had been altered, and the autopsy records and the autopsy X-rays had been faked. Lifton did, in fact, discover fairly early on 'a crucial piece of evidence', as the thesis I am discussing suggests – an FBI memo written at the time of the autopsy, which referred to medical work done on the president's head, which contradicted the official autopsy report. This clue lead him into 15 years research.

And such clues are still being discovered by studying the evidence. Last year someone in the States went through the Warren Commission 26 volumes and wrote down all the biographical data on Oswald scattered through them. Assembled together it showed that there were quite clearly two people called Lee Harvey Oswald being described; two people, of different sizes, in different schools, in different parts of the United State at the same time. Quite what this means, I don't know.[1]

And after the murders of the sixties there followed Watergate, Iran-Contra, Koreagate, Whitewatergate, the CIA-cocaine story and all the rest. Within this strand of what is thought of as conspiracy theory the model of an ordinary Joe finding a clue fits only the assassinations. The other great scandals have been researched chiefly, but not exclusively, by journalists, and deviant academics, like Peter Dale Scott. However, it would be a mistake to think of people like Scott or Lifton as conspiracy *theorists*. Like the other serious Kennedy researchers, they barely deal in theories at all. Their work is entirely, even obsessively, empirical.

The thesis I took as my starting point consisted of three parts. First, it posited the existence of something called conspiracy theory lore, two of the main strands of which I have discussed. The second part of the thesis was that central to this lore is the idea that some 'crucial piece of evidence is uncovered by some ordinary Joe'. This has been true occasionally. Finally, the thesis suggested that there is a dichotomy between the intricacy of the plans and the way details of the plans leak out to the public. It is to this suggestion that I now turn.

Treated strictly, the proposition that 'details of the *plans* leak out to the public' is simply false. This never happens. The examples of individuals, ordinary members of Joe Public, finding clues all have the same feature: the existence of the conspiracy is revealed not by flaws in the *plan* but in deceptions which conceal, and the cover-up which follows, the event. Whoever killed the Kennedys and King got away clean: the conspiracies weren't detected and have still to be officially acknowledged.

What has changed since the 1960s is the delay between the conspiracy and its detection after the event; and, more importantly, the process of then getting the media to pay attention. Take the Oklahoma bombing of a couple of years ago. The official version of that started to come apart within weeks of the explosion; chiefly, I think, because of the intensity of the media interest. With hundreds of journalists converging on such a scene these days, dozens – even hundreds – of people get interviewed on air, large chunks of it get recorded on videotape for later analysis and comparison; and it is not possible to put a clamp on what is broadcast as it was in the 1960s. As a result, a lot of information 'escapes' and it is then impossible to persuade the media entirely to accept the cover-up line. To get back to the thesis I started with, in the Oklahoma bombing, individuals watching the torrent of media coverage began to notice discrepancies in the reporting. Loose ends weren't tied up. Witnesses appeared with divergent testimony: people who heard more than one explosion, or who reported that the Alcohol, Tobacco and Firearms personnel had all left the building before the bomb went off. And far from being supported entirely by 'anoraks', the most striking testimony in the Oklahoma bomb case that I have seen, has come from a retired US Army munitions expert, who, after examining the explosion and damage, concluded that it couldn't have been made by a van full of home-made, fertilizer-based explosive: it simply wouldn't have produced the blast necessary to destroy the buildings' internal supporting pillars. For a rough comparison, look at the Oklahoma pictures and then look at the pictures of the damage caused by the IRA bombs in the City of London in the early 1990s. The IRA bombs blew in a lot of building fronts and windows but didn't do anything like the structural damage of the Oklahoma bomb.

The thesis I began with asked, 'If these conspirators are so clever how come the crucial piece of evidence is uncovered by some ordinary Joe?' Are conspirators clever? In the case of big events like the assassinations of the 1960s, the Kennedys and King, the conspiracy hinged on presenting the forces of law and order with a ready-made solution. Oswald was framed, but framed so crudely it is pretty obvious he was meant to be a dead assassin. What they had against him would never have stood up in court; and had he appeared in court he would have talked of his various intelligence roles. Before his apprehension, Oswald *was* nearly shot. At the point of arrest in the cinema, a policeman did try to shoot him but the gun misfired. At that point, Oswald began screaming, 'I am not resisting arrest', and the police then felt unable to kill him in front of the dozen or so people in the cinema audience.

In the killing of Martin Luther King, the police were again involved. The patsy was run round America, told to buy a rifle, and finally installed in a boarding-house near the site of the shooting. The police detailed to guard King were pulled off and King was shot. The rest was easy because the local police found a rifle and other bits and pieces with James Earl Ray's name on them, conveniently left near the scene of the crime. Voila! Case closed: everybody in Memphis law enforcement was happy. Everybody, that is, except the black cop who had been guarding King, who had been called away just before the shooting. James Earl Ray, threatened with the death penalty if he was tried and convicted, accepted a plea bargain, and confessed to something he hadn't done. So there was no trial: the evidence against Ray was not tested. Again, as with the JFK murder, there was no serious investigation by the authorities.

With the Robert Kennedy murder, it was more sophisticated. In that one, the patsy assassin was actually witnessed shooting at Kennedy, while the actual assassin, dressed as a security guard, did the deed standing behind Kennedy. The American system's refusal to take on board the RFK assassination is even more perverse than in the case of his brother. The autopsy evidence is absolutely clear that Robert Kennedy was shot at point-blank range behind his ear: his skin had power burns suggesting a firing distance of inches. Which means it couldn't have been Sirhan, who was in front of him; which means it had to be someone who was behind him. On being shot, Robert Kennedy whirled round and tried to grab the security guard. Robert *Kennedy* knew who had shot him.

How competent were these conspirators? Pretty competent, you'd have to say. The official verdicts remain that Oswald, Ray and Sirhan did the deeds. The major American media were persuaded by their connections to the CIA to accept the 'lone assassin' verdict in JFK's case; and having compromised themselves once, were not inclined to ask awkward questions about the other two killings.

All three assassinations hinged on corrupt local police forces either co-operating with the murders or not doing their jobs properly. All three relied on the major media and the political system not to ask questions. It is one of the striking political facts of American history that the Democratic Party lost its two most charismatic leaders and never generated much of a head of steam for a decent inquiry. Had it not been for the handful of 'anoraks' back in the sixties poring over the Warren Commission evidence, the whole thing would have slipped into history just as Allen Dulles predicted.

I was going to say that I doubt any of these assassinations could take place today. But the Sirhan Sirhan scenario seems to have been used a couple of years ago in Israel in the shooting of Yitzak Rabin: patsy firing blanks while somebody else does the real shooting. But in the US, the climate has shifted profoundly, due in no small part to the work of the little group of 'nutters' in the sixties who refused to be silenced by the government. And there is too much media interest these days. In 1963/4, once the major media had been cooled off, that was it. These days there would be dozens, if not hundreds, of independent and competing TV reporters looking for a new angle. Look at the feeding frenzy which has developed over something as piffling as Bill Clinton's sex life, for example.

The current contender for the description of conspiracy lore or tradition, and one which might even seem to fit the model of an ongoing conspiracy which has been discovered by ordinary Joes, is the great UFO-alien-secret contact-abduction-government-alien deal-cattle-mutilation-Majestic 12-back engineering-secret bases-Area 51-black helicopter mystery. About this I am reluctant to say much, mainly because I don't feel that I've read enough. However, it seems to me that there is genuine mystery here; or, rather, a number of genuine mysteries. I know that most of those writing for *Fortean Times* and *Magonia*, for example, have pretty much concluded that the extra-terrestrial hypothesis, has been completely discredited. I don't accept this: nor, I'm pretty sure, do the organisations of the US government which monitor the world's air space. Too much official US government paper has been uncovered which shows that the US government's organisations have taken a very keen interest in UFOs, and do not believe they are dealing with some kind of psychological or folkloric phenomenon. Psychological and folkloric phenomena do not leave radar tracks, do not buzz aircraft and US or Soviet air force bases, all of which has been thoroughly documented.

However, the concrete existence of literally *Unidentified* Flying Objects, or Fast Walkers, as I believe they are called, in current US Air Force parlance, is really not the issue here. The conspiracy theorists in this area believe something much more striking is happening than that there are UFOs whizzing about beneath the Van Allen belt popping down once in a while to freak out the natives and pick up a few souvenirs. They believe in a vast government conspiracy not only to deny knowledge to the US population – this bit I think is true; but then governments deny their citizens all kinds of knowledge – but also in a variety of theories which claim that:

- the US government and the aliens did a deal in the post-war years;
- that various secret committees have been involved in this;
- that the aliens, in their part of the deal, gave the US government access to advanced technology;
- that alien space technology – either back engineered from retrieved crashed UFOs, or from the alleged deal in the late 1940s with the US government – is being used to develop strange craft at Area 51 and other alleged secret locations.

Initially this looks like a good candidate for the description of 'a lore', I think; a body of traditions and facts on a subject. Unfortunately the evidence for most of this is – let's be generous – weak in the extreme. There are relatively few uncontested facts; and some of the crucial 'facts' in this area, the Majestic 12 material for example, seems to have been conclusively demonstrated to have been fabricated. And many of the theories barely deserve the description of 'a theory' at all. Nonetheless there is a torrent of stories in this area at the moment in US and UK UFO magazines. In America, one or two of the allegations come from named sources and make claims about their careers inside various bits of the government. When journalists report back that there is no trace of them having worked at NASA, say, the sources reply, 'Ah well, the records have been erased.' This is almost certainly, but not absolutely certainly, baloney. Such erasing of documents does go on; and with so much data now kept on computer, is increasingly easy to do. This makes it impossible to absolutely, conclusively, dismiss X or Y.

This UFO conspiracy material is expanding and elaborating very fast at the moment. In the British UFO mags in the last couple of years we have had a stream of tales of secret bases, dead bodies all over the place, and secret army units running round the UK cleaning up the mess. Some of the claims are not that far removed from a British version of Will Smith and Tommy Lee Jones in the Men in Black movie. In all these stories, the sources of information are anonymous; all claim to be serving or former military personnel. And, oddly enough, all have decided that the best forum for their extraordinary, earth-shattering story is not the *News of the World*, let alone Panorama or the House of Commons, but a British UFO magazine. One researcher I know was even rung up by someone claiming to be a London taxi-driver, who proceeded to tell my friend the hoary old story about the government official who had left his briefcase full of secret documents about the aliens and government in his cab. Given that my friend is ex-directory, he wondered how a London taxi-driver had got his number. The documents were not forthcoming, of course.

I presume this is all disinformation. That it gets into print at all is either a testimony to the *gullibility* of many of the people producing UFO mags, the *cynicism* of such people, or 'perhaps' simply the shortage of decent material to fill monthly publications.

We know there are government disinformation programs being run in this field in the United States. Linda Moulton Howe, who made the film Strange Harvest, about the cattle mutilation phenomenon, unwittingly took part in one. She told the journalist C.B. Bryan how she was invited to the Kirkland Air Force Base. In the Air Force Office of Special Investigations there, she met one of its staff who told her that her film had 'upset some people in Washington'. As a result, his superiors had asked him to brief her. She was shown a document called – wait for it – *Briefing Paper for the President of the United States on the Subject of Identified Aerial Vehicles (IAVs) – IAVs*. This contained a history of US Government retrieval 'of crashed discs and alien bodies, dead and alive'. The Roswell incident was just one of several. But Howe was not allowed to make notes or copies of this document, just to read it.

Does this scenario sound vaguely familiar to anyone? It should, because this is precisely the disinformation technique used by Colin Wallace in the British Army's psy-ops unit in Belfast in the 1970s. Wallace would take journalists, especially foreign journalists with a limited understanding of British politics, into a back room and show them 'secret documents' which they could read but not copy. Some of the documents were genuine, some forgeries. We have copies of some of the forged documents which show that Wallace's unit, with information from MI5, was faking documents with which to try and link the Labour Party to the IRA.

Alas, when Ms Howe was given the same treatment, no warning bell seems to have rung. This is rather odd really, for here was the US Air Force apparently deciding to let her in on the story they had spent so much time and money previously trying to deny or rubbish.

In offices in the US and the UK, there are groups of psychological warfare wizards planning this nonsense and then feeding it out. Perhaps they run bets, among themselves, these psy-war wallahs, just to make the job interesting: bet you ten bucks you can't get *this* published. But, alas, these days there is almost nothing you can't get published in some part of the UFO publishing field.

As to what they're doing? One hypothesis I have seen for this current explosion in the UK, is that such stories would act as cover for the flying of experimental US aircraft in and around the UK. There is a precedent: in the 1950s, the US government encouraged the idea of UFOs to provide cover for the secret U2 spy plane program. When people saw a bright light in the sky – the sun shining on the U2 at 35,000 feet – they remembered the story in the local paper about the UFO seen in the next county. But if *you* had experimental, secret aircraft, would you fly them up and down the Irish Sea? Or in the vast almost unpopulated deserts of Arizona, New Mexico and Colorado, or over the Pacific ocean?

My guess is they're just muddying the waters; making the whole subject look utterly ridiculous in the hope that the major media will never take any of this great cluster of subjects seriously.

And so we have arrived at the smart-asses employed by our governments. For the most important of the sources of conspiracy in our societies are the secret organisations of the state. Here I do detect a faint memory of what I said two years ago. All states run security services and intelligence outfits of one kind or another. All conspire; all, in a sense, simply *are* conspiracies. MI5 currently claims to employ around 2000 people full-time. You may wonder what they are doing now they don't have the Soviet Trade Mission to keep them busy. Working against terrorism, organised crime and drugs, apparently. Has the price of heroin and cocaine dropped since MI5 got involved? Not that I've heard. MI5 tell us they no longer have anyone keeping an eye on British subversives. But how would we know? With the exception of a tiny amount of PR work in the last few years, and the identity of the last two MI5 Director Generals, the rest of their work and their personnel is officially secret. At any rate secret to us, until someone blows the whistle, something goes wrong; or, as in recent years, bureaucratic turf wars break out with other government agencies, in this case the police.

MI5's struggle with the police over terrorism provoked both sides to engage in a war of leaking to, and briefing of, the media, as MI5 tried to show their political masters what a clever, efficient organisation they are, and why they should be given this or that role. And the police tried to show that it was dangerous to give this unaccountable organisation these areas. (As if the police were accountable!) At the end of this media war, MI5 had grabbed part of the terrorism turf. Most of the stories about MI5's activities in the past five years have come not from some 'ordinary Joe' discovering a clue, but from MI5, via their tame British journalists.

The total number of state employees in the world currently engaged in secret work – what we might call officially sanctioned conspiracies – must run into millions. Of their activities, only a fraction of 0.1% is ever exposed. Reading any spy memoir, for example Peter Wright's *Spycatcher*, or the recent books about the CIA spy Aldridge Ames, or the revelations last year of former MI5 officer David Shayler, always reveal activities, operations, to which we – Joe Public – were oblivious at the time. So: for the most part, state conspiracies are very successful in the sense that very, very few are ever exposed; and even fewer are exposed close enough to their taking place to prevent the plan of the conspirators being put into effect. And of the tiny handful of state conspiracies exposed to public view, few if any fit the model of discovery by some 'crucial piece of evidence uncovered by some ordinary Joe', allegedly to be found in conspiracy lore.

So, are conspirators competent? It is tempting just to say yes, those working for the state certainly are: they're still unchallenged, their budgets are still intact; careers, pensions and gongs still on track. Their clients are still in power. But how competent do they need to be? Given the power to arrest and harass, backed-up by the state's monopoly of violence, a half-wit could run such operations; especially when, in this society, all the opposition can muster is the National Council for Civil Liberties, a handful of MPs, one or two journalists in the major media, and magazines like mine which hardly anybody reads. As I'm sure I said two years ago, these are the important areas we should be looking at. The UFO-alien conspiracy-abduction frenzy is fascinating; but the British American Project for the Future Generation contains four members of the current British Cabinet.

Finally, a caution about the use of the concepts of 'anorak' and 'trainspotter', meaning pathetic, sad, obsessed, irrational. I used 'anorak' in what I've just said, and I shouldn't have. 'Anorak' and 'trainspotter' are concepts used and popularised in recent years by journalists to denigrate people with longer attention spans than their own. Most journalists' idea of research is nipping down to the cuttings library and having a quick squint, or making a couple of phone calls to someone half a step ahead of themselves. Most of them work on stories for hours rather than days; let alone weeks or years. A part of them knows this isn't good enough and they fend off this uncomfortable thought by dismissing those with deeper or longer interests as anoraks, obsessives, trainspotters, hobbyists, and, the really useful one, 'people with an agenda'. Journalists are intensely suspicious of people with agendas – even if, perhaps especially if, that agenda is the truth about something.

Even though most of what the anoraks among us uncover turns out to be crap, let's not just sneer at them.

Anoraks, at least, are trying. We should encourage the anorak in all of us. It would just be so much better if the anoraks could be persuaded to think a little more clearly and check things a little more carefully.

Notes

1 This is a reference to John Armstrong who eventually produced an enormous (1000 pages plus a CD-Rom of evidence), self-published, barely edited book on the subject, *Harvey and Lee*, in 2002. The book is fascinating but it exemplifies some of the worst characteristics of self-publiciation. The book can be bought at <www.armstrong.jfkresearch.com>. Better, in the first instance, to Google 'Harvey and Lee + John Armstrong' which will produce extracts from the book and talks Armstrong has given on the subject.

A SLOW MOTION COUP:
THE BRITISH WATERGATE

CHAPTER SEVEN

What will America do if Labour wins? The lessons of Australia and New Zealand

CND Conference in Coventry, 1986.

Let us assume that Labour wins the next election and decides to actually implement its current policy of expelling US missiles. What could the US government do?

The present Labour leadership appears to believe, or pretends to believe, that they will do nothing. I think they're wrong. I think we have to assume, on a worst case basis, that the US government means it when they say that they see the Labour Party's policies as a serious threat to NATO; and this being so, we have to assume that they will seek to prevent such policies being implemented

What this might mean I can only speculate, but some recent experiences in this country and Australia in the middle 1970s, and New Zealand recently, offer some hints of the kinds of reactions we might get.

The significance of the New Zealand and Australia experience at the hands of imperial America is that they are, in so far as these categories mean anything, white, English-speaking countries. The history of the post-WW2

American empire is one coup after another run against recalcitrant brown and black peoples from Guatemala to Grenada. But, for most people in this country, perhaps because we are members of a racist society still encumbered with the garbage of empire, these examples, these plain facts of post-war history, don't count. After all, we aren't a Chile or a Dominican Republic, are we? Whatever our actual status in the world – a banana monarchy, perhaps? – we are . . . what? A Western democracy – yes; and underneath that, we are white (mostly) and English-speaking (mostly). We are not a Third World country. But neither are New Zealand and Australia, also mostly white and English-speaking; and New Zealand is currently being destabilised by the US government; and in 1975 the Gough Whitlam government in Australia was dismissed, removed, by the US government, its partners in the ANZUS alliance. The parallels with the UK are that much more acute because, in both cases - Australia in the 1970s and New Zealand today - it is mild social-democratic Labour Parties, like ours today, and I mean that simply as a description, not a value judgement, which posed the 'threat' to US interests.

By 1975 when Governor Kerr, the representative in Australia not of the British government, but of the Crown, dismissed the Whitlam government, at the behest of the CIA, the Whitlam government had become a threat by:

- asking questions about CIA funding of the opposition party led by Malcolm Fraser;

- asking questions about CIA operations and installations inside Australia;
- checking the small print in some of the military and intelligence treaties between the two states;
- exploring ways of raising the capital to buy out some of the US multinationals which own large chunks of the Australian economy.

To the US government it was a considerable indictment – the Aussies were actually beginning to pursue an independent version of the Australian national interest. So, in the end, the CIA called Governor Kerr, who, as it happened, had once worked for a CIA front; and Kerr called in Whitlam and sacked his government. The ultimate US threat was to cut off the Australian intelligence and military from US intelligence – for the spooks and the generals, the equivalent of being cast into the outer darkness. The very next day, Governor Kerr did his duty.

Incidentally, although I haven't yet looked at this very closely, I get the impression that this bizarre colonial event took place with barely a murmur from the British Labour government of the day. The passivity displayed by the Thatcher government before the US invasion of Grenada was displayed in 1975 by the Labour government

Gough Whitlam's recent court appearance in the Peter Wright trial looks to me very much like revenge for events of 1975. Mr Kinnock might have learned more useful things had his staff made 8 calls to Gough

Whitlam last week rather than calling Peter Wright's lawyer. Perhaps they did. It would be reassuring if it were true.

Fortunately for the British Labour Party, if it choses to make use of the opportunity, US actions against New Zealand are recent and ongoing. We can actually watch a US campaign against a white, democratically elected, genuinely popular government.

The first thing worth pointing out is that the New Zealand government's policies, which have so provoked the US government, are insignificant in comparison to those proposed by the Labour Party. Labour Party policies may seem pretty tame stuff to the would-be revolutionaries amongst us, but they are downright radical compared to New Zealand which just wanted to exclude nuclear-powered and nuclear-armed warships – a gesture about as strategically significant as Hull declaring itself nuclear-free. However, gesture or not, the New Zealand government was first cut-off from US and UK intelligence sources, and then effectively expelled from ANZUS – an unprecedented act against a member of a US alliance since the war.

A large number of US-funded groups are now working inside New Zealand to undermine the government. This list will be largely meaningless in the time I have to describe them – I have written about this in more detail in an article which should appear in February's issue of the END Journal. However, just to get a flavour, if nothing else, here is the list I have to date.

Inside the New Zealand labour movement are the Labour Committee on Pacific Affairs, funded by the US Information Agency (USIA); the Asia-America Free Labour Institute, also funded by the USIA, one of four overseas training institutes jointly run with the CIA by the AFL-CIO, more or less the US equivalent of the TUC; and the USIA-funded Australian and New Zealand Labour Leader project.

At the political level, there is the Pacific Democratic Union, an informal alliance of right-wing political parties in the Pacific, funded by the US via the National Endowment for Democracy (also currently funding the SDLP in Northern Ireland). The New Zealand equivalent of the Tories, the National Party, is the New Zealand representative in the Pacific Democratic Forum.

The Georgetown Centre for Strategic and International Studies, one of the key centres of the regenerated Cold War, has recently set up an ANZUS think tank. At its head is the former Deputy Director of the CIA, Ray Cline. Cline is one of the senior US figures who has long been associated with the World Anti-Communist League, and Cline has recruited into his ANZUS think tank one of New Zealand's best known far right-wingers, one Bruce Larsen, a long-time member of the World Anti-Communist League. The World Anti-Communist League and its Asian equivalent, the Asian Peoples' Anti-Communist League, have, to date, attracted the support of four National Party MPs.

Another prominent feature of the new Cold War, the Heritage Foundation, has also been down under, with three members visiting, writing reports and powwowing with the New Zealand Right. One of the three Heritage people was Richard Allen, Reagan's first National Security Adviser, who resigned when he was caught taking a bribe. For the Heritage Foundation the diagnosis is easy: Moscow is behind it all.

There have also been a rash of US academic 'experts' with intelligence or State Department backgrounds on visits, and a number of conferences on the ANZUS question.

USIA money is also being used to support a number of new groups which have 'spontaneously' developed in New Zealand: the Plains Club, the Senate, the Campaign for a Soviet-free New Zealand, and Collective Security Inc. There are also a couple of Moonie fronts operating there now.

All this, mark you, in a country with a population the size of South London; and this list is simply part of what the New Zealand peace movement has identified. What is going on covertly, no-one knows. What the good old CIA is up to, no-one knows. They will be doing something. One attempt to create a CIA front company in New Zealand was exposed last year when the parent company went bust in Honolulu.

The US is hardly going to attempt to run a coup against New Zealand on the Chile model. They hardly need to risk the bad publicity. They will simply change New Zealand public opinion. Enough money and enough pressure, and the opinion will change. New Zealand is not strategically significant and the US can afford to sit and wait for the next general election there. All they have to do is ensure that the Lange government loses – or changes its policies.

And finally there is Britain, the Wilson government of 1974-76 and their adventures with MI5. Briefly, for those who haven't read my account of this in *Lobster* 11, led by MI5, a disinformation and destabilisation campaign was run from 1974 through 1976 against the Labour government, the Liberal Party and Mr Heath and one or two of his closest political allies. This cabal wanted a right-wing Tory government to stand up to the Left and the unions. Jeremy Thorpe got smeared with the Norman Scott material and Peter Hain got prosecuted for bank robbery. The Labour Party endured two years of sustained leaks, smears, rumours and forgeries – and bugging and surveillance courtesy of Mr Peter Wright and his buddies in MI5's black bag unit.

This campaign failed to bring down Wilson, but succeeded in discrediting the Liberals, played a part in ridding the Tory Party of Heath, and succeeded, triumphantly, in the end with the election of Mrs Thatcher, an old-fashioned red-hunter, the 'enemies within' and everything, as leader of the Tory Party in 1975. Though I can't prove this yet, my opinion is that a large number of apparently separate events between the two elections of 1974, the peak of this activity – the rumours of coup plotting by the Army, the formation of various 'private armies' and the attempt to kidnap Princess Anne, for example – were all co-ordinated elements in a 'strategy of tension'. All of which leaves us where, today?

I can't say what will happen to the next Labour government, but there are lessons to be learned from New Zealand today and the UK and Australia yesterday. I think there is a better than 50% chance that the MI5 scandals of 1974 and 75 will eventually bring down this government. But that will only happen if the Labour Party abandons the absurd pretence of this bipartisan agreement on security. This is the most important big lie at present, because for most of this state, and all of the secret state, preventing the Labour Party doing anything significant is the essence of 'security'. That's what 'security' means. The security services are there to ensure that the Left in general and the Labour Party in particular, fails. To have the Labour Party wedded to this is preposterous. With any luck, Mrs Thatcher will do a New Zealand on Kinnock and cut him off from the security briefings he's been getting, thus ending the bipartisan nonsense once and for all.

The best defence the Labour Party has against future destabilisation campaigns is to go hell for leather and expose the 1974/5 model. I don't expect the CIA to attempt to destabilise the Labour government, not when there is MI5 in place with 50 years of experience – successful experience – to do the job for them. Certain Labour MPs are deeply interested in this and I have high hopes at present that the whole stinking mess will be dragged into the light. Exposing past calumnies *may* take the sting out of MI5 for the future. May . . .

The second thing the Labour leadership ought to do is reduce the threat their policies pose to US interests. The

British and American Right just don't believe that a Kinnock-led government could be trusted. In the back of their minds is the belief that after Kinnock got elected, a la GLC, there would be a palace revolution and the Marxist/Trotskyist Left in the party would run a putsch against the leadership and, hey presto, we would have a Soviet-style regime in this country. It's laughable, of course, but that is what they are afraid of. If you want to try out this scenario, it is at the heart of Frederick Forsyth's novel *The Fourth Protocol*, the core sections of which Forsyth has acknowledged he got from MI5. They are conveniently printed in italics.

I don't believe it is possible to change the Right's mind on this. No amount of 'reasonableness' will work. After all, in 1974-76, it was the Tribune Group of MPs which the Right perceived to be the threat, Neil Kinnock included. His name was on a list of 'dangerous subversives' put out by the then Social Democratic Alliance, led by Stephen Haseler, in 1976. Kinnock may be a right-wing shit to the British Left, but to the Right he is a dangerous man. And comparing Labour's defence policy to what it was in the 1970s, you can see some sense in this view. The Labour Party, certainly in its foreign and defence policies, just is much further to the left than it was in the seventies.

So how do we reduce the threat we pose to US interests? Start from scratch. All the parties' policies, all the positions on what will happen after the US missiles are expelled, share the same fault. They claim to be able to predict the future. Labour claims the future is benign: Britain's defences will be enhanced, NATO won't be damaged, the Soviet Union won't start rattling their nuclear weapons at us. The Right says the opposite. None of them, any more than I am, are capable of predicting what will happen. None of us know, none of us *can* know. It's all bullshit, waffle, castles in the air. Foreign policies are uncertain: prediction impossible – which is why states employ spies. Spies are employed to find out what other states are going to do – usually without success. Thus Labour Party claims about the post-US missile expulsion world are as stupid as, but no more stupid than, anybody else's.

The way out, the way of having a more intelligent policy and the way to reduce the perceived threat, is to say, 'Yes, we will expel these missiles and see what will happen. If any of the disastrous consequences predicted by the right take place – if Soviet submarines do start appearing in the Thames, say – we will invite the missiles back again.' The attractions of this policy are immense to me. By acknowledging the unavoidable uncertainty of prediction, this policy makes all the policies which claim predictive powers look asinine – which they are. It provides a neat defence from attack from the Right. You say, 'Well old boy, you might well be right, why don't we give it a whirl and see what actually happens.' Best of all, it offers a way of actually empirically testing some of the fundamental questions about geopolitical reality. What will the Soviets do? Here's how we find out. Suck it and see.

My final point to those who find the idea of having a conditional commitment to sending back the US missiles horrifying is this: what difference could it possibly make? If a war breaks out, we will get attacked as long as we have US bases and US communication systems in Britain. The missiles are simply a symbolic gesture. Their presence on, or disappearance from, these shores makes not a jot of difference to the actual safety of this country. (And if the nuclear winter hypothesis is true, even with no US bases here, if a war breaks out and nukes are used, we all die anyway.)

So let's start treating the missiles and their return as the symbolic gesture it is; but let's also use their expulsion not to make ourselves feel righteous but to find out what political reality actually is. This chance of empirical investigation of Soviet behaviour strikes me as the only really important consequence of sending back the US missiles. Of course, it may be precisely this which makes the Right nervous. Maybe we send them back and nothing awful does arrive from Moscow. Either way, wouldn't it be interesting to find out, once and for all?

Comment

It is curious to see how optimistic I was in 1986. We might bring down the government! Abandoning the bipartisan approach to the intelligence and security services was something the Labour Party never considered, any more than CND considered adopting my suggestion of a suck-it-and-see policy on the US missiles. And how incomplete was my view of the 1970s. It became clear quite soon after this talk was given that the events of the mid 1970s were not solely or even predominantly the work of MI5, but of a loose alliance of serving and former intelligence and security officers, some retired military, and assets in the media and big business. I discussed this in my talk to Chesterfield Labour Party, included in this collection, the following year, and it is one of the major themes of the book I co-wrote in 1991, *Smear! Wilson and the Secret State* (Fourth Estate).

CHAPTER EIGHT

Towards Rational Paranoia

Talk given to the END (European Nuclear Disarmament) Conference, 1987.

In this country, we are about to begin a Watergate-type experience, thanks to Harold Wilson, Peter Wright and Colin Wallace. On the Watergate analogy we are somewhere in late 1973 or early 1974. The outline of something is visible: all we have to do is join up the dots and await the outcome of the final scenes.

As the opponents of state policies of NATO member countries, the peace movement is, *de facto*, the enemy of those states; and those states, and their intelligence and propaganda arms, have tried, and will continue to try to undermine, manipulate, infiltrate, attack and, when they can, destroy us, collectively and, where convenient, individually.

It seems to me that if we are serious – and our opponents within the state structures are very serious indeed – we have to become as expert on them, who they are, how they operate, as they undoubtedly are on us. I can't speak for other European countries, but in Britain this is a fairly daunting process. Our ruling elites have been in power a long time and have employed tens of thousands of people to ensure that they stay there. Which is to say, it is bloody hard to find out what is actually going on in this country. It is true that we know a great deal more than we did even five years ago but we are still ignorant about many of the most basic building blocks. For example, what is the Cabinet Office? How big is it? What kinds of powers does it have? I don't know: there appear to be no books or articles on the subject. To me it begins to look like an embryonic version of the National Security Council, the apparatus that Ollie North has been playing with. But who knows? And yet the Cabinet Office staff are the people – some of the people – we would deprive of that most addictive of drugs, their power. Know thine enemy? We haven't really got a clue, and that may explain why they win and we lose.

On the whole, states behave the same way. The political police, the military bureaucracies, the intelligence agencies here, use the same methods and rationales as spooks, bully boys and generals everywhere else. There are only so many ways of finding out who is doing what to whom, and how to prevent or manipulate it. When Kim Philby defected, he presumably didn't have to go to school to learn how the KGB operates: he knew that already because it operates the same way that SIS does . . .

The similarities between the intelligence agencies of the apparently competing world powers may explain the stream of anecdotes from retired CIA officers which describe how this or that officer, posted somewhere in Asia or Africa, ends up getting friendly with his or her KGB counterpart. And why not? They are professionals. They understand each other's work and its anxieties.

They are each other's most important peers. Of course they can get to be buddies. As members of the elites from super powers they probably share the same basic contempt for the rest of us; and few of them seem to take that political bullshit very seriously any way, do they?

Because states and their palace guards are pretty much the same the whole world over, we can generate useful insights and hypotheses about how *this* secretive society works by looking at the experiences of other people – New Zealand for example, the land of the well preserved Morris Minor, whose political and social structure seems to be very similar to ours.

I got interested in events in New Zealand a couple of years ago when the first reports appeared here which suggested that the US was taking a serious interest in New Zealand's anti-nuclear policies. I remember going round to talk to Peter Crampton[1] – we live near each other in Hull – to talk about New Zealand and its relevance to the British anti-nuclear campaign. I wrote to some people in New Zealand, began collecting the material, and discovered that New Zealand had been getting the treatment from a range of US state organs, including the good old CIA. The names of these fronts, the sources of the money, the people on the New Zealand Right who have been used to launder it, hardly matter here: they're just a lot of names which will mean nothing out of context.[2]

The point about New Zealand is that here is the US state, with the CIA as the symbolic ultimate bad guy, doing pretty much the standard operation to change the government of a country whose policies are in conflict with Uncle Sam's. We are used to the US doing their heavy dancing on black, brown and yellow peoples. There is a long catalogue of known operations with the CIA as the cutting edge in Africa, Asia and South and Central America. New Zealand's importance is that it is a white country (with no disrespect to the Maori people), an English-speaking country and, indeed, let us not entirely forget, a Commonwealth country. And CIA operations against us white folks are relatively hard to find: a few in France and Italy, especially in the immediate war years; a publishing front in Britain; but really very little.

I'm not sure whether the paucity of information on CIA operations in Britain, for example, means that so far they have just been lucky and gone undetected, or that there are just relatively few of them, with the CIA leaving this country to our own spooks. Even if the latter is generally true, the presence of Cord Meyer as head of the London CIA station during the mid 1970s suggests they were up to something serious during that period. Meyer is top drawer, A1, CIA big cheese, one of their top operators and founder members. Whatever he was actually doing, it wasn't watching British television.

To return to New Zealand . . .

Peter Crampton and I wrote a little piece for *Tribune* suggesting that maybe we – in our case we meant the Labour Party and the anti-nuclear movement – might learn something from New Zealand: in 1986, basically, what might be in store for a unilaterally inclined Labour government. In the event the Labour Party doesn't seem to have even noticed what was going on down there. If a Labour MP, let alone a member of the Shadow Cabinet, has visited New Zealand since 1985 he – or she – has done it very quietly. Remember the internationalist, Commonwealth-supporting Labour Party? Well it – we – have managed not to even notice that the anti-nuclear New Zealand Labour government has been under attack by the US for the past 3 years, let alone say or do anything about it.

This shouldn't come as a surprise: it was a British Labour government, apparently in control of the British state and the levers of power which, in 1975, did nothing – probably didn't even notice – that the Australian Labour government of Gough Whitlam was being removed by the American state, led by the CIA.

Even though the New Zealand government has received the full weight of the US state's persuaders in the past three years, the signs are that it will survive. Last I heard, Lange's government seemed set for re-election, the anti-nuclear policies were still genuinely popular. I don't know the situation there well enough to say why Uncle Sam has failed down under, but my guess is that part of the explanation may be found in the 1986 'Libyan scare' mounted by the US in Vanuatu, the little group of islands off the north east coast of Australia.

As manufactured Cold War incidents go, the Vanuatu 'Libyan scare' was pretty ineffectual. Farcical even. In the first place, as journalists quickly discovered, there were no Libyans on Vanuatu. But the point really is to look at the fact that Libya rather than the Soviet Union had been chosen to play the role of the bogey man. For in that part of the world it seems peculiarly difficult to create a convincing Soviet or Chinese 'threat' – because, of course, there isn't one; and without that basic conceptual tool it is just too hard to create a plausible rationale for doing what Uncle Sam wants. The other reason for the failed US campaign in New Zealand may be that the New Zealand Left had taken the lessons of Gough Whitlam to heart and were waiting for the US to start work on them. The result has been a very impressive series of revelations about US operations there. Knowledge may be power.

In this country, alas, a reasonably plausible Soviet 'threat' can still be generated, even if it gets harder and harder to bring the corpse back from the edge of death. Even in the early 1970s, when Colin Wallace was working for the British state in Northern Ireland, so inadequate was the actual Soviet 'subversive threat', MI5 was forced to invent one. Indeed, so desperate were they for any real events to use, that a figure as insignificant as the Trotskyist Ernest Mandel, on a trip to Eire to talk to some young socialists in 1972, was pumped up into a major step into the KGB's insidious take-over of Britain via our own Cuba, Northern Ireland.

This fantasy Soviet 'threat' reached a grand climax with the claims that Harold Wilson was a KGB agent. Poor old Wilson. Everybody left of the CIA agents in the Labour Party thought he was a right-wing shit, while the Right said he was a KGB agent. Poor old Harold Wilson had the classic paranoid's experience: he really did know what was going on and nobody believed him. Most farcical of all, honest, loyal Brit and slavering Royalist that he is, he has since played the game and kept his mouth shut. He won't talk about the political police in this country even though they tried to topple his government.[3]

Rereading the newspapers of the 1974 period now, it is incomprehensible to me that so few members of the Parliamentary Labour Party had any sense that something odd was going down. Almost weekly there was some new scandal, real or manufactured. 1974 remains a monument to the irrepressible naiveté of the Parliamentary Labour Party and the British Left as a whole. As far as I can remember, only the Workers Revolutionary Party seemed to have any sense of what was going on; but their paranoia about the British spooks was buried under their hysterical analyses of the approaching economic disaster. I remember the WRP's newspaper in 1974 predicting 13 million unemployed. The point remains, however, that a slow motion coup was being run in 1974 and 5 and barely a soul noticed.

We have to get geared up, get better informed. We all have to become experts on the ways of the state, and especially the secret state. They are going to continue bugging, tapping, opening mail, forging documents, planting agents, creating phoney groups, running campaigns, subsidising people on the right, manufacturing and spreading dirt. This is the nature of the beast.

Our political police began in earnest in the 1880s. Let me recommend Bernard Porter's recent history of the early years of the Special Branch. It makes very instructive reading. In the 1880s, instead of a Soviet 'threat', they had – and helped to manufacture – an anarchist 'threat'. They will always find an enemy. I have already commented on the use of the Libyan 'threat' in Vanuatu, and the new candidate they seem to be preparing for another big push is the international terrorist threat. The appearance this year of the Institute for the Study of Terrorism suggests this to me. Watch out: we are certainly in for more 'international terrorism', real or manufactured.[4]

We have to pay attention and educate ourselves. Then we have to educate the Parliamentary Labour Party, few of whom know anything about this area. Had they been elected this year, they would have gone like lambs to the slaughter, incapable of really believing that the British state would just basically fuck them over.

We have to always bear in mind the late Ralph J. Gleason's fundamental law of American politics, formulated during Watergate: no matter how paranoid you are, what they're really doing is worse than you could possibly imagine. Because of Gough Whitlam's fate, the New Zealand Left and peace movement seem to have made the shift into rational paranoia. Until we do likewise, I'm afraid that the bad guys will go on running rings around us.

Notes

1 At that time, one of the founders of END, later MEP for Humberside.

2 See the previous essay for some of the details.

3 At this time, we didn't know that Wilson had Alzeimer's disease. We now know that it was probable that he didn't talk because he couldn't remember. Wilson

resigned in 1976 at the onset of Alzeimer's. His father had it and he suspected he would get it too.

4 I cannot claim prescience here. A number of sources, including, I seem to remember, the *Daily Telegraph*, reported on a big conference held in Israel in 1979 at the Jonathan Institute – essentially a front for Mossad – at which a group of American, Israeli and British intelligence officers decided to run two big themes: (a) push USSR as sponsor of the world terror threat (out of which came the KGB-shot-the-Pope nonsense) and (b) identify Palestinians as the local Soviet-sponsored Arab terrorists.

CHAPTER NINE

The Lessons of Spycatcher

Talk given to Chesterfield Labour Party, 1987.

Now *Spycatcher* is a very interesting book in many ways but if anyone here is thinking of buying it to learn more about the plot against the Labour government of Harold Wilson, don't bother. Everything – and that isn't much – he has to say on that subject is included in *The Sunday Times* extracts of some months ago. There are no names in that section of the book, though via *The Observer*, Wright has leaked some of the names to Dale Campbell-Savours MP, thus into Parliament and Parliamentary privilege, and thence into the newspapers. Put all the clippings together and you can construct a sort of expanded Peter Wright version of the plot.

But Peter Wright, even the reconstructed Peter Wright, isn't telling us the truth. He says it was a plot against only the Labour Party, and yet we know from other sources that it was wider than that – and he must know this too.

One of these other sources is Colin Wallace, the British Army's psychological operations officer, who was working in Northern Ireland during this period. We know from him not only that the plot was aimed at the Liberals and the Heathite Tories, but also some of the smears that MI5 were trying to get established.

On the content of the disinformation campaign, we have Wallace, receiving dirt from MI5 in London; and we also have *Private Eye* for that period. For it is now acknowledged that throughout its existence it was the recipient of MI5 information and disinformation. A look through the pages of the Eye for the period 1970-75 shows dozens of pages, some of them the same smears that were being run through Colin Wallace in Northern Ireland. This episode in the *Eye*'s history is discussed at some length in Patrick Marnham's new book about Lord Lucan, *Trail of Destruction*.

A third source, of course, was one of the chief victims, Harold Wilson. He talked at length to Barry Penrose and Roger Courtiour, and though the resulting book The *Pencourt File*, was a mess, nevertheless there is a good deal of interesting information in it. Penrose, incidentally, now with *The Sunday Times*, is rewriting that book at the moment in the light of the revelations of last year.[1]

A fourth is Gordon Winter, the BOSS agent, and his book *Inside BOSS*.

Here we are, 8 years into the counterrevolution of the Right; and it may be difficult to remember that in the early 1970s many of the ruling class in this country believed that they were on the edge of a left-wing revolution, laughable though that may have been. I don't want to try and précis those complex years but a few of the headlines of the period should bring it all back: Heath's U-turns, the miners' strike, 3-day weeks; advice about bathing by candlelight. For our masters in their big country houses in the South it may well have seemed like the end of the world as they knew it: the lights were, literally, going out all over the Home Counties. The great devils, Jones and Scanlon, were thought to be on the verge of taking over. Here's a splendid quotation from the Heath Cabinet member, John Davies, describing how he saw things in December 1973.

'We were at home in Cheshire, and I said to my wife and children that we should have a nice time, because I deeply believed then that it was the last Christmas of its kind we would enjoy.'

For many on the right, I think, the events of the early 1970s were merely the final confirmation that there could be no middle way, no compromise between capital and its opponents; their anxieties about the Labour Party and the Labour movement which had always been there, appeared to be realised. Thus the reconstruction of British politics, along pre-Second World War lines, was undertaken; and undertaken covertly. It isn't, as Wright tells us, that a group of disgruntled MI5 officers decided to try and remove Wilson. It was a loose alliance of British and foreign intelligence agencies, finance capital, and right-wing ideologues which worked (a) to discredit the Labour

Party (b) discredit the Liberal Party and (c) to discredit the 'wet' Tories. As early as 1972 one of the key players in this, the former SIS deputy director, George Kennedy Young, had written of Heath, 'the Queer will be overthrown'.

The alliance of intelligence agencies includes BOSS, Rhodesian intelligence, MI5 and the CIA. They were all running disinformation and smears. On the fringes of this were various military people like David Stirling and General Walter Walker, preparing – or apparently preparing – to take on and destroy the unions, the so-called private armies of 1974, GB75 and Civil Assistance. (I don't think these groups were seriously intent on this confrontation with the unions; they were psychological operations, part of what we ought to call a strategy of tension in this period.)

The ideologues, with considerable input from intelligence agents like Brian Crozier and Robert Moss, began reconstructing the intellectual climate. Milton Friedman was dug up from somewhere and awarded the Nobel Prize. Freedom and the money supply became the order of the day. Moss and Crozier helped get the Freedom Association, initially called the National Association for Freedom, off the ground. And the replacement of Edward Heath with a right-wing leader was organised by Edward Du Cann, Airey Neave and others – with assistance from the ubiquitous George Kennedy Young.

If all this seems difficult to get hold of, the best advice I can offer is go back to the period just after World War 1 when exactly the same thing happened. The right feared the rise of Labour and socialism; there were strikebreaking 'private armies' created; an enormous number of right-wing pressure groups appeared; MI5 and the police were working hand-in-glove with the entire range of anti-Left forces – and the great showdown feared by the Right was avoided. The 1926 general strike was the end of it, rather than the climax: the real events had all taken place before. In this period there was even something which looked very like the SDP – the British Workers' League – which fizzled out as as soon as the crisis passed. If you read the 1920s stuff first, understanding the 1970s is quite simple. Only the names of the groups have changed . . .

Notes

1 This rewrite never appeared. Many years later Simon Freeman put together some of the Penrose files on the subject and produced *Rinkagate*, a reworking of the Norman Scott–Jeremy Thorpe story.

CHAPTER TEN

The Wilson Plots

Talk given in the History Department, Newcastle University, 1999.

'The Wilson plots' is a portmanteau term for a collection of fragments of knowledge about intelligence operations *against* the Labour governments of Harold Wilson and a great many other people and organisations. 'The Wilson plots' is about a good deal more than Harold Wilson and his governments. I won't attempt to describe this complicated area but merely offer a sketch.

The British state – and the secret state – had never trusted the British Left and had always worked to undermine it. The Attlee government came out of the wartime coalition and was considered mostly safe and reliable by the state: and by safe and reliable I mean it did not seek to challenge either the power of the state nor the assumptions about the importance of finance capital, the British empire and Britain's role as world power which underpinned it.

Harold Wilson, a most conservative man, made one

large mistake while a young man as far as the state was concerned: he was not sufficiently anti-Soviet. During the 1940s and 50s, while many of his Labour colleagues were accepting freebies from the Americans and going to the United States for nice holidays, Wilson was travelling east, fixing trade deals with the Soviet Union. He was perceived by the secret state – by some sections of the secret state, notably but not exclusively, sections of MI5 – to be someone who, in the words of the late General Sir Walter Walker, 'digs with the wrong foot'. In short, Wilson was perceived by some to be a dangerous lefty and his arrival as leader of the Labour Party was thought by some of the professionally paranoid Cold War Warriors in the British and American secret states to be deeply suspicious. Wilson had been to the Soviet Union many times. Was he a KGB agent, they wondered? Had he been entrapped and blackmailed?

Asking that question was enough for MI5 to begin obsessively investigating Wilson and his colleagues and friends. Nothing was found. But to the professional paranoids, nothing found simply suggested it was better hidden than they first thought. And so they carried on.

Meanwhile, the Left in Britain was on the rise: trade unions got more powerful. The professional paranoids, noting the influence of the Communist Party of Great Britain in some trade unions, began to see the shift leftwards in the UK in the sixties and early 1970s as somehow under Soviet control. In 1973/4, Conservative Prime Minister Heath had his fateful showdown with the miners union – and lost – and the Tory Right and their friends in the secret state began a series of operations to prevent what they believed – or pretended to believe – was an imminent left revolution in Britain. Some of these operations were done by the secret state; some by people close to but not in the secret state. Bits of the CIA also shared this view and got involved. And the South African intelligence service, then called BOSS, the Bureau of State Security, was running parallel operations against Labour and Liberal politicians it perceived as South Africa's enemies, notably the Liberal leader Jeremy Thorpe and the then leader of the Young Liberals, now the Labour MP, Peter Hain.

It is worth noting here that similar operations were being run in this period against mild, reformist, leftish parties in New Zealand, Australia and Germany, in Canada against the Quebec separatists, and, most famously, in Chile.

This extraordinarily complex period of British history saw covert operations of one sort or another involving serving or former personnel from MI5, MI6, the CIA, Ministry of Defence and the Information Research Department, *plus* assets in the media and the trade unions, *plus* allies in the Conservative Party and the City. That it tends to get summarised as 'MI5 plots against Wilson' is due to the way the information about these areas emerged in 1986-88, through former Army information officer, Colin Wallace, and the former MI5 officer, Peter Wright. They both talked about MI5 as the source of plotting against Wilson (though Wallace's allegations were much wider than that) and for much of the left-liberal media and politicians in this country, this fitted straight into their vague understanding of the intelligence services and British domestic history which told them that the bad guys were MI5. By the time we had educated ourselves sufficiently to understand what Wallace and Wright were saying, the perception – the false perception – that the story was just MI5 plotting against the Labour government had been established.

It is largely now forgotten that the first attempt to get 'the Wilson plots' story going was made by Wilson himself. Harold Wilson was aware of the various attempts to get the media to run smear stories about him and his circle, and aware of the stream of burglaries afflicting himself, his personal staff and other Labour Party figures in the 1974-76 period. But he chose to do nothing in public while he was in office. In private, he tried to get the Cabinet Secretary, Sir John Hunt, to do something, though what Hunt did is still unknown.

It seems clear now that Wilson did nothing publicly for four reasons. The first was that he didn't have anything substantial to go on – merely suspicions and a lot of little wispy bits and pieces of rumours and tip-offs. The second reason for his inaction was his distrust of MI5. Had Wilson instructed Whitehall to do an inquiry, it would have turned to MI5; and it was MI5 that Wilson and his personal secretary, Marcia Williams, suspected of being at the root of their troubles. The third reason Wilson did nothing while in office was his knowledge in 1974 when he won the election, that he would only serve two more years and quit. Wilson, we now know, was afraid of what was then called senility, now called Alzeimers: it had afflicted his father and he told his inner circle in 1974 that he was going to resign in 1976 when he was 60. In 1975/6, ensuring a smooth hand-over of power to his successor – and Labour was a minority government, don't forget – was a much greater priority than finding out who was behind the burglaries of his offices and the rumours about him. Wilson was a loyal member of the Labour Party to which he owed everything. He didn't want to make bad publicity for the Party and his successor. The fourth reason Wilson did nothing, was his memory of the previous time he had tried. In his first term in office, encouraged by George Wigg MP, he had tried taking on the Whitehall security establishment in the so-called D-notice Affair and had got his fingers badly burned.

As far as we know, Wilson had very little real, concrete, information about what was going on in 1976 when he retired. He knew that he and his circle were being repeatedly burgled. He had watched the campaign being run against Jeremy Thorpe, the leader of the Liberal Party, by the South African intelligence service, BOSS, and that is why he made his first public remarks not about MI5, the objects of his real suspicions, but about BOSS. But those comments produced all the negative reactions he feared – not surprisingly, since he had almost no evidence – and he let it drop until he resigned.

He then waited a couple of months and contacted two journalists, Barry Penrose and Roger Courtiour, who became mockingly titled Pencourt, gave them the little he had and hoped for the best. But without any decent leads into the MI5 material, PenCourt stumbled – or were led; it isn't clear which – into the story being run by the South African intelligence service, of Liberal leader Jeremy Thorpe and his brief affair with Norman Scott, not the story of MI5's campaign against Wilson. There was a brief flurry of interest by the media, notably by *The Observer* which had paid a lot of money for the serialisation rights to the PenCourt book, but nothing happened and the story disappeared. Wilson tried to get his successor James Callaghan to do something but Callaghan declined.

The story disappeared for two reasons. The only journalists or politicians in the late 1970s who knew anything about the secret state were currently or formerly employed by the secret state or were mouthpieces for it. There was no investigative journalism in 1978 in the UK worth mentioning; there were no former British intelligence officers to show journalists the way; there were no whistle-blowers, no renegades. There were no courses being taught in universities. There were almost no books to read. In 1978 the British secret state was, really was, still secret.

After the failure of the PenCourt investigation, nothing happened for five years. Harold Wilson became a Lord, presided over a long inquiry into the City of London which was consigned to the recycle bin as soon as it was published, and duly developed Alzeimer's as he suspected he would. His personal assistant for 30 years, Marcia Williams, became Lady Faulkender and has said nothing of consequence since. Barry Penrose and Roger Courtiour made a lot of money. Penrose is now just another hack, last seen working for the *Express*. Courtiour is in the BBC somewhere.

By 1979 the extraordinary events of the 1974-76 period – events which, let me remind you, included *The Times* seriously discussing the right conditions for a military coup in the UK, and a considerable chunk of the British establishment wondering if the Prime Minister was a KGB agent – had just slipped by, unexamined. In came Mrs Thatcher, with her GCSE understanding of economics, who proceeded to wreck the British economy, creating 2 million unemployed in 18 months, and the entire story – or group of stories we know as the Wilson plots – simply ceased to be of interest to all but a handful of people.

One of that handful was Colin Wallace, who in 1980 began a ten year sentence for a manslaughter he didn't commit. Wallace was interested in the Wilson plots story because he had not only been a minor participant in the plots, and had knowledge of other areas of secret activities, he knew he was in prison to stop him talking about them. The other interested party was the former MI5 officer, Peter Wright. He had also been a participant in the plots and had also been maltreated by his erstwhile employers in the secret state. Not framed and imprisoned like Wallace, but denied a decent pension on a technicality after a lifetime's service to the state.

Here is one of the outstanding lessons of this episode. The British secret state is an astonishingly inept employer of people. None of those who became well known whistle blowers in the 1980s and 90s, Wright and Wallace, John Stalker, Captain Fred Holroyd, Cathy Massiter, David Shayler and Richard Tomlinson, wanted to be whistle-blowers. They were converted into whistle-blowers by the stupidity of their employers in the state. Wallace, Holroyd and Wright, for example, were loyal Queen and Country men to a fault, right-wingers through and through. Unfortunately, our secret state has only one response to internal dissent or the possibility of public revelation of its own errors: smash, crush, smear, destroy, frame, cover-up and lie. The secret state perceives itself to be defending the national interest and in the national interest anything is permitted.

In prison in the 1980s, Colin Wallace began writing letters about his wrongful conviction and accounts of his experiences working for the British Army's psychological warfare operation in Northern Ireland. In that capacity, he had witnessed some of MI5's attempts to smear Wilson and other politicians as communists, drug-takers, homosexuals etc. The major media took no notice. Duncan Campbell at *The New Statesman* did take notice but had an enormous amount on his agenda. So Wallace ended up working with Steve Dorril and me instead.

Despite Wallace's allegations made while in prison and published by me in *Lobster* and distributed all over the British media in the months preceding his release *from* prison, the media took almost no notice. They only sat up and paid attention when the first rumours about a book being published in Australia by a former MI5 officer called Peter Wright began circulating in the UK. One nut-case talking about the Wilson plots could be ignored; two, apparently, could not.

I want to say something here about how the secret state tried to frustrate Wallace's attempts to get his story out. We now know, from a former senior civil servant called Clive Ponting – another whistle-blower in the 1980s – that in the months before Wallace's release from prison, the Ministry of Defence set up a committee, with MI5, to deal with him. It is worth noting here that this committee did not simply order his murder. Outside Northern Ireland, our secret state seems to kill people very rarely. But it is also worth noting that the committee was set up to pervert the course of justice. *Precisely* what this committee did is not known, but its general remit was to discredit Wallace and so discredit his allegations. Two of its operations were detected and they show what can be done with unaccountable power.

Colin Wallace was a skydiving enthusiast and eventually the Army in Northern Ireland began including skydiving in its psychological operations. Wallace formed a free-fall team which did displays all over Northern Ireland and was used to try to create positive feelings about the Army – basic hearts and minds stuff. Wallace's speciality was descending dressed as Santa Claus and giving out presents to kids. Wallace the parachuting Santa.

Skydiving in this country is very tightly controlled: every jump is recorded by the British Parachuting Association. As you do more jumps, you get differing kinds of licenses: beginners, intermediate, advanced – that sort of thing. Wallace had an advanced, 'D' license. Or so he said.

By mid 1987, despite the huge amount of space devoted to the allegations filtered back from Australia from the Peter Wright book, *Spycatcher*, there were only three groups of journalists trying to research the complex tales Wallace told: Channel Four News, where I was briefly; David Leigh and Paul Lashmar at *The Observer*; and, a bit later, Paul Foot at the *Mirror*. Other journalists dropped in and out, did odd stories, but only those three groups were seriously at it. We all had the same basic problem: Wallace had been described as a 'Walter Mitty' by Ministry of Defence briefings during his trial in 1980 and the Ministry of Defence was simply denying that Wallace had the job he said he did in Northern Ireland. Wallace claimed to have had access to secret intelligence material in his capacity as a psy-ops officer for the British Army. Since the psy ops unit was officially deniable, i.e. officially didn't exist, the MOD line was that Wallace was simply a press officer – his official, public role – and the rest was fantasies. We were trying to establish the veracity not only of his claims about events but also his claims about his own CV.

In the summer of 1987, rumours began spreading through this little group of journalists that Wallace's claims to have been a skydiver were a fake. He was a fantasist, a Walter Mitty. These rumours arrived at

Channel Four News via an old colleague of Wallace's who knew an ITN journalist. The rumours seemed inexplicable at first: we had lots of pictures of Wallace skydiving with and without his Santa Claus outfit. But when I finally rang the British Parachuting Association to check their file on Wallace, I found they had no record of him. Eventually Paul Foot, also working on the story, discovered that a duplicate set of records were held by the international parachuting body and Wallace's records were there, confirming that he was what he said he was – as far as skydiving went, anyway.

Undaunted by this, a journalist still ran the 'Wallace-is-a-fake' parachuting story some months later in a double page spread in *The Independent* smearing Wallace and Fred Holroyd. The point here is, we can now work out some of what this MOD-MI5 operation against Wallace consisted of. First, they picked one area of Wallace's CV, his parachuting, and set out to discredit him with it. If they could show he was lying here, they believed, journalists would not believe his other claims. They burgled his house and stole his jumping log book; they burgled the British Parachuting Association and removed his file, substituting a fake file for the one with his number on it. Then they began spreading the word through their press contacts that Wallace was a fraud, knowing that Wallace didn't have his jumping log and knowing that – eventually – some journalist would ring the British Parachuting Association and ask about his record. Finding nothing, because his file had been removed, such a journalist would consider the allegation that he was a fantasist proven and would thus dismiss him as the 'Walter Mitty' figure described at his trial. In effect, the MOD tried to convert Wallace into the 'Walter Mitty' they said he was. Unfortunately for the MOD, Paul Foot was a better journalist than that and found the duplicate set. Without Foot we would have been struggling to rebut the Wallace-is-a fantasist line.

Another disinformation project about Wallace was fed through Professor Paul Wilkinson, then at Aberdeen University. A former RAF officer, Wilkinson was ITN's official consultant on terrorism. Somebody in the MOD or MI5 fed him some material about Wallace which accused him of trying to get a man in Northern Ireland killed so he – Wallace – could have the man's wife. This smear story had been created just before Wallace left Northern Ireland – presumably in case they ever needed to get at him. Wilkinson wrote a letter, passing this derogatory material on to ITN. Fortunately, by this point, Channel Four News's management were pretty sure Wallace was telling the truth, and showed us journalists Wilkinson's letter. The allegations it contained were refutable, and Wallace wrote to the university authorities.

The point here is this: Wallace had already been framed for manslaughter and convicted in a rigged trial. Having failed to shut Wallace up with six years of imprisonment, the secret state then set about discrediting him. If you could get to the people on the MOD/MI5 committee which planned this and asked them why they were doing it, they would simply say it was in the national interest to prevent Wallace talking. In the minds of the secret state, the national interest – as defined by them – overrides the competing claims of justice and democracy.

I offer these anecdotes by way of introduction to some comments on the relationship between the media, politicians and what we might call historical truth. Many people vaguely assume, as I did at the beginning of the Wallace affair, that politicians and journalists are concerned with 'the truth'. This simply isn't the case. Most journalists – at least 99% of those I have met – are interested first in their careers, and aims subsidiary to that, such as getting a story or doing better than their rivals; or having a good time or padding their expenses. Journalists are just people doing a job. They have mortgages and families to support; and theirs is now a very insecure business. All the unions in the media were smashed in the past 15 years. Contracts are short. You can be fired on the spot.

Politicians, most of them, are simply interested in power or aims subsidiary to that, such as getting re-selected, getting re-elected; pleasing the whips to get promotion; or simply getting press coverage. The pursuit of the truth is not on the agenda of most politicians; the pursuit of the truth, when it means going against prevailing media opinion, or the wishes of their party's leaders, or the wishes of the state, is on the agenda of a handful. This is particularly true of stories in the field of intelligence and security policy. Nothing makes MPs more nervous than security and intelligence issues.

In the first place, if they've got half a brain, MPs

simply won't go near subjects about which they are ignorant – which is sensible enough. And to my knowledge, other than those who have worked for, or have been close to the security and intelligence services, there are no MPs who have a decent knowledge of this field. Not even Tam Dalyell. In the second place, MPs all have a healthy respect for the damage to careers tangling with the spooks can inflict. You might think that MPs then have a massive vested interested in bringing the security and intelligence services under their control. But this hasn't happened yet and, in my view, short of some massive, earthshaking scandal, never will.

In the House of Commons in 1987, we got some help from Ken Livingstone, Tam Dalyell and Dale Campbell-Savours. These days Dalyell is still at it, as is Norman Baker, a Lib-Dem MP, a new member of the so-called awkward squad. Livingstone has moved onto other areas and Campbell-Savours has become a Blair loyalist.

The British political and media systems are not equipped to deal with major issues concerning the behaviour of the secret state.

In the political arena the Intelligence and Security Committee set up under the Tories is a joke, without investigative powers. But it is a joke useful to the secret state. When the House of Commons Foreign Affairs Committee was conducting hearings into the Sierra Leone affair last year, it asked for an interview with the head of MI6. Foreign Secretary Robin Cook denied them access on the grounds that the Security and Intelligence Committee was the appropriate forum for such questions. MPs are still unable to ask questions about the Security and Intelligence services: the House of Commons Clerks simply will not accept them. The secret state is still, officially, not accountable to Parliament.

At its heart, the Wilson plots story was the attempt by a handful of people to persuade the major print and broadcast media and parliament that their view of the British political universe was false. I was writing articles which implied: you – the media, the politicians – do not know what you are talking about; the world isn't the way you say it is. At the beginning, before the major media took any real interest in the Wallace story, this was a peculiarly difficult message to sell. Who was I to tell experienced journalists they didn't know what was what? I was on the dole, living in the sticks, in Hull, producing a magazine with a tiny circulation.

In the weeks before Wallace came out of prison, I had circulated a great deal of material to the major media about Wallace, his case and his explosive allegations. I got only one response, from a journalist at Newsnight. As big-time journalists are prone to do, he said, don't tell me over the phone, come down to London. So down to Newsnight's office went my erstwhile partner in *Lobster*, Steve Dorril, and I. It was our first exposure to the major media. We delivered the spiel and the journalist was interested and said he would take a camera crew down to the prison to interview Wallace when he got out.

We had been told by Wallace that among the visitors to his secret psy-ops unit, Information Policy, in Northern Ireland, had been Alan Protheroe, who at the time of our

Newsnight visit, was Assistant Director General of the BBC. Nicknamed 'the Colonel' in the BBC, Protheroe was, and may still be, a part-time soldier-cum-intelligence officer, specialising in military-media relations.

But unlike the journalists we had been talking to up to that point, Protheroe knew who Wallace was and what the Information Policy unit had been doing in Northern Ireland. To Newsnight we therefore said something like this: 'Protheroe's a spook; you'll have to watch him. He'll try and block anything you do with Wallace in it.' 'Really, old boy,' said the BBC people we were talking to, 'It isn't like that in the BBC.'

Their response was comical, really. It was then only just over a year since there had been several weeks of intense media interest in the revelation that the BBC actually had its own in-house MI5 office vetting BBC employees (still there, as far as I know) – *prima facie* evidence that, *au contraire*, the BBC was exactly 'like that'.

The Newsnight journalist, Julian O'Hallorhan, interviewed Wallace the day he came out of prison and then had his piece yanked out of a programme at the very last minute. I was actually watching Newsnight at the time and saw the confusion in the studio as the running order was rejigged while they were on air. We subsequently heard that Protheroe had indeed blocked the Wallace interview, and when asked, the BBC denied that they had ever interviewed Wallace. (Paul Foot has seen a bootleg of the film-which-didn't-exist.) Protheroe's action in blocking the Wallace interview was reported four months later in the *Sunday Times* and has been confirmed since by a senior Newsnight staffer who has now left the BBC.

Thirteen years later, have things improved? Yes and no. The media is potentially more difficult to manage for the state than it used to be. The Ministry of Defence employs 150 press officers to spin-doctor the media and even MI6 has a media department whose job it is to wine and dine journalists and editors to get the departmental line across. The days when a quiet word in the ear of a handful of editors would ensure a media blackout are gone. And there is a good deal more information available than there was in 1986 – if journalists could be bothered to read it – which, mostly, they can't.

But the fundamental attitudes of the media towards the state and secret state remain the same as far as I am aware. British journalists – and, more importantly – British editors, do not see themselves in an adversarial relationship with the state and secret state. If the secret state says 'national security' to them, most journalists and virtually all editors will still back away. And in some ways the situation today is even worse than it was then. Investigative journalism is expensive, offers no guarantee of publishable articles, or broadcastable TV programmes, and there is less of it now than there was then. There has been a visible dumbing-down of the few TV documentary series, such as World in Action, into consumerism programmes. Not counting the journalists who are simply mouthpieces for the state, there is currently only one journalist in the whole of Britain who is seriously interested in the intelligence and security field, and that's Paul Lashmar at *The Independent*.

And his very interesting and important book about the Information Research Department, which came out last year, to my knowledge has attracted almost zero attention.

In 1990, I think it was, a resolution of mine became the North Hull Labour Party's conference resolution. It called for a full-scale public inquiry into Northern Ireland, the dirty war there, the Wallace affair and the Wilson plots; it called for the introduction of a system of real parliamentary accountability for the secret state. The resolution went to the Labour Party conference where it was passed without opposition. As such, according to the rules of the Party, it became party policy. Of course nothing happened, the whole thing has been forgotten and we are where we were in 1986 before the Wilson plots story got going. Short of a bug being found in Tony and Cherie Blair's bedroom with 'please return to MI5' stamped on it, New Labour is not likely to challenge the secret state – and maybe not even then.

Although Britain is a democracy in some senses, the 'will of the people' has never been extended to cover the key areas of interest to a state which was developed to run and service an empire. Defence, foreign policy, security and intelligence policy – in none of these areas can MPs or their constituents have access to official information or have any input into policy. During World Wars 1 and 2, the state co-opted the mass media of the day for its propaganda; and this continued to some extent after the War in the Cold War with the Soviet bloc when large chunks of the media were co-opted again to run anti-

Soviet propaganda. This is what is described in the new Paul Lashmar book about the Information Research Department; and is presumably the reason it has been so widely ignored.

At the end of the day, as the cliché has it, it's down to the politicians. As long as the politicians remain content not to have any influence over foreign and defence affairs – and the intelligence agencies which service them – the media will remain relatively impotent and the subject will remain off the agenda. And, unfortunately, this present intake of Labour MPs shows every sign of being at least as supine before the state as those who came before it.

CHAPTER ELEVEN

How the British Media Failed to get 'the Wilson Plots' Story

Talk given to a meeting organised by the Campaign for Press and Broadcasting Freedom, Manchester, 1988.

How many working journalists have we got here? Well, I'm not a journalist. I've really only had two months journalistic experience as a temporary researcher with Channel Four News. But I was lucky enough to be there doing the MI5 plots stuff, while there was a good deal of activity by the higher media on this story last year. And I want to draw on this tiny bit of experience to make a number of points.

We are drowning in information. I can no longer read the stuff that's appearing. But this is still a very secretive society – more accurately, perhaps, a very secretive ruling class and spectacularly secretive state machine. And the closer you get to the heart of it the more secretive it gets. This is a contemporary banality.

For the British media to go about a story like the Wilson-MI5 plots, is to push very close to the core of our rulers' secrets. This is a big no-no.[1] There are those who insist that the British media are useless, have no political bottle, flunk the really hot stories. They were wrong last year. Almost everybody had a crack at the Wilson plots story. Panorama did, Central TV did, Yorkshire TV did. World in Action, I was told, were maintaining a watching brief. Channel 4 News did. Newsnight got in early and had their first piece on it yanked by Alan Protheroe. *The Guardian*, *Observer* and *Sunday Times* had various teams on it. Insight was reborn and worked on it. I met some of these people at the very early stages of their projects. It was exciting. Under a Tory government, a nasty repressive Tory government, the serious British media set about researching a story whose outline all the journalists knew and, I think, knew to be true: that this administration was a result – direct or indirect, depending on how tough a version you assemble – of a series of conspiracies involving the secret heart of the state. It was your basic fantasy left-wing story: MI5 and the Tory Party and the City of London and the CIA and BOSS working to screw the Labour government.

So, early last summer, all this money, all these talented TV people set off to hunt down and fetch THE story back to their bosses. And none of us did. Yorkshire, in first, very early, quit when other people joined in what had been their exclusive. Central went off to America, I think, and got nothing of importance on the CIA angle and quit. Panorama had their project stopped – precisely why isn't clear to me. Newsnight, having had their knuckles rapped by Protheroe right at the beginning, months before anybody but Yorkshire was interested, as far as I know, never returned to it.

We couldn't do the story. Nobody would talk – or if they would talk they wouldn't talk on the record. The secretive society triumphed – yes. But there was something else going on, another factor which, a year later, seems to me to be more important than I realised at the time: there was no political support for the research. In other words, the Labour Party, the Parliamentary Labour Party, flunked it.

Maybe there is someone here who was involved in one of the other areas – that would be good – but I want to describe what happened at Channel Four News. We actually got something on the screen by concentrating on the one person who was talking – talking to anyone who would listen, Colin Wallace. In truth while we talk of the Peter Wright story, most of the energy last year went into Colin Wallace's version. He was here – Wright was down under, and not talking.

We did a series of pieces, the last of which included Wallace's connections with Airey Neave at the time when Neave was Mrs Thatcher's right-hand man. As we approached Mrs Thatcher and the Tory Party, the rumbling unhappiness with all this inside Channel Four News mounted. And in the end, you know what was being said? 'Look, no-one's interested; there's nothing in the papers.' Which was true. It wasn't a story because people were not standing up in the Commons and repeating it. The only support we had was from Ken Livingstone. Great guy: I admire him. He's the only Labour politician who's ever taken the story as seriously as it deserves – i.e. it is the most important story in British domestic politics since WW2. But support from Ken alone is not what you want. Loony Ken, loony story. It's easy.

What seemed like a secrecy problem was also a political problem. Without the feedback from the politicians, we couldn't keep it going. The odd thing is that last June both of the following propositions were true and defensible inside Channel Four News: this is not a story; this is the biggest story since WW2. The reporter I was working for, Robert Parker, once part of World in Action here, had worked 14 hours a day, six days a week for three months on it, needed a rest, took a summer holiday and when he came back . . . the management had lost interest . . . whatever. It doesn't matter. The next thing on our list had been Kincora, one of the really massive subsidiary scandals in this saga which no TV programme has ever tried to do.

But the end result last year was that the only TV coverage of the Wilson-MI5 plots were a handful of pieces on Channel Four News. Nothing else has appeared since, despite thousands of column inches of printed journalism.

TV political journalism works within the context of British politics. It's another banality, yet very important. With a Tory government and the British state doing its damnedest to keep the lid on this, running disinformation constantly, the story's survival depended upon the support of the Opposition to validate it as 'a story'. This didn't happen – and still isn't happening. Labour MPs, with about 4 or 5 exceptions, don't understand this story, don't have time to read the material, and, as politicians, are not going to stand up in the Commons and start blathering on about things they aren't sure of. Investigative journalists in this country are horribly handicapped by the state of the Labour Party in the House of Commons.

I'm not saying that there was anyone else about to break out of the woodwork last summer – maybe one – to support Wallace (and Wright) but the political climate sure wasn't a help. An imaginary conversation: 'Hey, why don't you go public with what you know. We can guarantee the public support of Ken Livingstone and, maybe, Tam Dalyell and even more maybe-ish, Dale Campbell Savours.' This would have been a hard pitch to make, especially to ex-military, ex-intelligence people who knew better than we did just what might happen to them.

We are going to see the Zircon film. In some ways what happened to Duncan and Zircon epitomises what I'm saying. Duncan exposed – tried to expose – a secret. The film was blocked – our secret society. Yet not a secret: we're about to see it. But more interesting, I think, is the fact that during the hassle about this film, Duncan was told by Neil Kinnock's press office to stop ringing them up. The Kinnock team were afraid that the Tory press would get to hear of it and the Labour Party would be presented as 'disloyal' etc. This, after all, was approaching the election. And the Kinnock camp got an awful shock when Mrs Thatcher went for Kinnock for allowing one of his staff to talk to Peter Wright's lawyer. They didn't want to know. Duncan didn't have the support of the Labour Party, even though the story was about Parliament being deceived by the state.

It is a secret society, yes. There are thousands of nasty secrets buried away, yes. But the Opposition won't take on board the few that get offered to them. That seems to me to be the problem. And I speak as a member of the Labour Party. A secret society, but one that has never been less secret; which has never been more creaky and leaking. The problem is, the political problem is, how to persuade our politicians to make use of this information.

One final thought for discussion. If we are going to accept, at some loose level, the thesis that in a capitalist society the media will reflect the interests of capital, last summer's media activity on the Wallace-Wilson-MI5 story alone means that the thesis is going to have to be pretty sophisticated – i.e. watered down – to include it.

Notes

1 I have occasionally been asked if I didn't feel frightened pursuing this subject. Frightened, no. Occasionally I wondered if I wouldn't get busted for something – breach of the Official Secrets Act, for example – but realised fairly quickly that in the event it would merely make me famous (or notorious) and would sell more copies of *Lobster*. And my guess would be that the secret state knew this, too, and thus did not harass me.

CHAPTER TWELVE

Labour and the Secret State

Tribune Conference, 'Labour in Power' London, 1989.

For the last couple of years I have been reading and rereading all the memoirs produced by the members of the governments of Harold Wilson and James Callaghan. The most striking impression I have had, especially in the last year, is the similarity between the 1963/4 period and today. The conflict on defence between the unilateralists and the multilateralists was resolved then with a Wilsonian fudge, rather similar to our current fudge: inheriting the Tory government's commitment to buy Polaris, Labour cancelled one of the four subs and bought the rest. As will happen with Trident – if we win the next election. Throughout 1963 and '64, the Tories were accumulating a large balance of payments deficit and before the '64 election, Wilson went round dampening down the expectations of the party and trade unions. The same thing is happening now – only the deficit is many times bigger, and the expectations I suspect, lowered by a decade of Thatcherism. In 1963/4, joining the EEC was starting to appear on the agenda – understood by hardly anybody, opposed by some, seen as a panacea by others; it would eventually be joined 'when the time is right.' Today we have the exchange rate mechanism – understood by hardly anybody, seen as a panacea by some; to be joined when the time is right.

In early 1964, Wilson and Patrick Gordon-Walker went to the United States and did a more or less secret deal with US bankers: support for the pound against City speculators. This year, Messrs. Brown and Smith have been to Paris and Bonn, presumably to line up the franc and the mark against the shysters and spivs in the City.

In 1964, the preceding years of Tory rule had been dotted with scandals involving MI5, notably the Profumo affair, which had damaged Macmillan. Wilson took office determined that Labour wouldn't get damaged in the same way. George Wigg was appointed as a kind of watchdog over MI5. But Wilson and Wigg knew practically nothing about the security and intelligence services – though Wigg fancied that he did – and in a series of skirmishes with them in the first Wilson government – phone-tapping of MPs, the D-notice affair, Rhodesia – Wilson and Wigg were outmanoeuvred completely. All Wigg appears to have been able to do was tighten up the vetting procedures. And MI5 responded to this helpful activity by working with the Tories, spreading disinformation about Wilson, Marcia Williams, Lord Chalfont (then, lest we forget, a Labour minister) and Uncle Tom Cobley and all – obsessively investigating the PLP for Moscow Gold and, not finding any, making it up.

In the past few years we've had Peter Wright, Cathy Massiter, Colin Wallace, Zircon etc etc. But there the similarities end. Where Wilson and Wigg used the security scandals of the sixties to harass Macmillan, the party leadership has done nothing with the torrent of revelations in the last few years, and appears to have no intention of doing anything if it wins the election. There is but one sentence in the Policy Review about Parliamentary scrutiny of the security services, and that will be forgotten about – if it hasn't been forgotten about already – when, if – we win the next election. If there is a member of the Shadow Cabinet who is keeping an eye on the spooks, or trying to understand their empire, I am unaware of him or her.

Yet in other Commonwealth countries, Canada, Australia, New Zealand, the spooks have been reined in, their powers reduced, their accountability to their nominal political masters increased – and for crimes which pale into insignificance compared to what we know has been going on here. So, why have our spokespersons so conspicuously turned their backs on the political gold mine represented by Wright, Wallace, Massiter, Fred Holroyd, the connections between the Thatcher wing of the Tory Party and the spooks, and so on, these past few years?

I think there are several factors involved here. The most important – and the most banal – is that this is a complicated subject which our leaders have avoided because they don't understand it and don't have the time and energy to tackle it. Hardly anybody, let alone a politician, is willing to tackle a gang of experts, in public, about something they don't understand. The only PLP members who have expressed interest to me have been the awkward squad – Dalyell, Campbell-Savours and Ken Livingstone, especially Ken; and even he hasn't had the time to learn the material, relying on other people to provide him with the ammunition to fire.

Ken's name also explains part of the disinterest of the PLP leadership. Anything he – or Tony Benn, for example – takes up, automatically becomes an anathema to the current leadership. In retrospect, Ken taking up the cases of Colin Wallace and Fred Holroyd in mid 1987 was just about the worst thing that could have happened. Any chance of activating anyone else with more clout disappeared as soon as he made his maiden speech in the Commons on these issues. This is not a criticism of Ken, by the way. It is the PLP leadership who have behaved irrationally over this.

Another factor explaining the passivity of the PLP in the face of the revelations of spook operations against democracy is, I think, just fear. This is one sleeping dog, they think, we don't want to kick. This is a mistake in my view. On past experience, this dog is going to bite them whether kicked or not; and it is a much less frightening beast once its behaviour is studied.

There may also be a feeling – and here I am guessing – within the PLP that there are skeletons in the party's cupboard which would be damaging if they were exposed. This, at any rate, is the line which is reiterated over and over again by the spooks' leading mouthpiece at present, X of the X. [Deleted for legal reasons.]. Well, there are, indeed, nasty things under the stone waiting to be revealed, but not of the kind Mr X keeps hinting at. Peter Wright and his ilk searched high and low in the sixties and seventies and found practically nothing. I do not believe that there is something dreadful they didn't use during the crisis of 1974. On the contrary, the skeletons awaiting exhumation relate not to Soviet but to American and British intelligence penetration and manipulation of the party and the unions.

This is a complicated subject and I have time only to hint at it. During the first Cold War, the Soviet and American blocs engaged in a massive and largely covert propaganda war for the political control of Western Europe. Soviet – KGB – fronts were paralleled by American and British – CIA and MI6 – fronts. The best known of these is the Congress for Cultural Freedom, CIA-funded, under whose auspices the Gaitskellite wing of the party blossomed during the 1950s. Another, now forgotten, was the World Assembly of Youth, WAY, funded initially by MI6 and then, after some argument, by the CIA. WAY did the usual things a propaganda group did: put out leaflets, magazines; organised and funded delegates to conferences and so on. WAY was just one operation in the struggle for the loyalties of the youth of Europe.

The same sorts of operations went on in the international organisations. The result is that there is a group of people who moved from the National Union of Students, or the International Student Conference, or WAY, or the

MI6-funded Ariel and Atlas Foundations, and who knows how many other 'educational' bodies, into the right-wing of the Parliamentary Labour Party and/or the EEC bureaucracy. Some of the details are in Bloch and Fitzgerald's book; others can be pieced together from bits and pieces.

Although the CIA-MI6 dimension to these bodies was well-known in the Soviet bloc – and publicised – it remained undetected in Europe or America until the mid 1960s. In 1966, just ahead of exposure of the CIA's funding of much of the world student political scene in *Ramparts* magazine, WAY was organised and renamed the British Youth Council. (I suspect, but have no evidence to support the view, that this reorganisation was done because the spooks knew that their luck would not hold much longer.) The British Youth Council is today still funded by 'the Foreign Office', whether that is a euphemism for MI6 I don't know, and also by the Department of Education and Science. In 1977, Charles Clarke was President of the National Union of Students and was chosen by the British Youth Council to join the organising committee of the World Youth Festival in Havana. The BYC chairman that year was Peter Mandelson.

These fragments of biography probably tell us nothing more about Clarke and Mandelson than that they were career-minded young men, politically sensible young men, with good connections. Mere membership of a body funded by the spooks or the Foreign Office does not mean that the individual members of that body knew anything about the funding, let alone were conscious 'agents'. There is nothing to suggest that Clarke or Mandelson ever wittingly met a member of the British and American intelligence services. Nonetheless it is curious and somehow symbolic that the two most important members of Neil Kinnock's entourage, Clarke, the gatekeeper, and Mandelson, the strategist, came into the party via the remnants of the student-youth movement which was almost entirely the creation of the Anglo-American intelligence community.

The organisational changes in the party are just beginning to smell of the bad old days of the 1940s and 50s when the party machine attempted to regulate the whole party from the centre; when US Labour attachés and Embassy information officers flitted round the party, dispensing advice, helping to fund journals, organising freebies to the United States for promising young members of the party and union movement.

If Clarke and Mandelson are guilty only of premature careerism, who are the spooks assets in Walworth Road and the Norman Shaw building? Whose rise through the party is being promoted by the 'friends' and their 'cousins'? Which members of the Wilson and Callaghan cabinets were briefing the London CIA station?

I would like to say that I have just digressed into the long-forgotten history of the Labour Party and the first Cold War. But to forget something, you have first to acknowledge its existence, and this has not yet happened. The history of the Labour Party and the British and American states and secret states in the first decade after WW2, have yet to be written. Some starts have been made by historians Anthony Carew in Manchester and Peter Weiler in Stanford. The point is this: the section of the party – and the wider Labour movement – which has the most to fear by a spreading awareness of the relationship between the party and the spooks is the Right, the Atlanticist wing. The real history of the first Cold War will not hurt the democratic Left: they – we, our antecedents – will be revealed as nothing more than rather naive about Stalinism. But the Right in the unions, the anti-socialist wing of the unions, and the Atlanticist wing of the PLP, will be revealed to have been hopping into bed with almost everybody from the CIA to the occasional British fascist holdover in their struggle with the Left in the party and the unions. There was no Moscow Gold in Britain during the first Cold War. Like Militant today, the CPGB raised its own money.[1] But there were dollars to be had.

While all these factors I have described play their part, at the heart of the PLP's unwillingness to contemplate tackling the secret empires of the spooks is a wider refusal to acknowledge that the British state just is the enemy of the Labour Party. (The spooks are merely the cutting edge of the wider state, what Anthony Verrier nicely called the Permanent Government.) I can understand a reluctance to acknowledge this. It is obviously much easier to believe that the Permanent Government, while it may have some anti-Labour biases, is a machine which a 'strong minister' can master. But however congenial this may be to some of the PLP, it is a mistake, as the diarists of the Wilson government show.

The general strategy of the party leadership appears to be to hoist the white flag, in advance, to all the groups which might attack it should it come to power. The absolute unwillingness to tackle the secret empire of the spooks manifested over the last three years is just an aspect of this general failure of nerve and imagination. If we win the next election it seems fairly certain that the Kinnock-led government, like Wilson's first administration, will be preoccupied with the economic crisis generated for it by the City of London, Exchange Rate Mechanism or not. Those of us who think that high on the agenda of such a government should be the reform of the British state and secret state will be as marginal then as we are now.

Notes

1 About this I was simply wrong. After the break-up of the Soviet empire it was revealed that the CPGB was indeed directly funded by Moscow – bags of used notes were given to the late Reuben Falber. This is discussed, for example, in the talk to the Islington Labour Party in 1996 included in this collection.

CHAPTER THIRTEEN

A Very British Coup

Campaign for Press and Broadcasting Freedom, Manchester, 1990.

The first thing that has to be said is that slowly Fred [Holroyd] and Colin [Wallace] are winning.[1] This is a remarkable achievement, really, and it has been a privilege to tag along with them. Not that taking on the British military-intelligence complex was a clever thing to do. You have to be pretty bloody stupid to think you can win against the MOD, MI5, the Cabinet Office, the RUC – and their allies in the media. This is a brick wall; but then some brick walls were designed for banging heads on. And there are some people, I'm happy to say, who are bloody-minded enough about certain principles – like the truth and democracy and justice – to keep running at the wall. Colin and Fred are not the only examples of this rare breed, of course; they just happen to be the ones I know.

With This Week on Thursday night, Hard News last night and the Media Show tomorrow all devoted to aspects of this story, this meeting could hardly have been better timed. I am sure this is a happy coincidence, though with a skilled operator like Colin, you never can be absolutely sure. These three programmes, coming within a week, represent an astonishing media turn-around in this story. I will never forget watching the BBC TV 9 o'clock news just after the initial announcement by the government at the end of January[2] when the lead item consisted of Colin, Paul Foot, Ken Livingstone and Tony Benn, all being taken seriously – 6 minutes of it. Neil Grant, Livingstone's researcher until recently – who is here and who has much to say – said that when Ken spoke after the government's initial statement, it was the first occasion when Ken was actually listened to by the House of Commons. In 1987, when Ken delivered his maiden speech about Wallace, Holroyd, Northern Ireland, Airey Neave and Mrs Thatcher, you would have got fantastic odds against Ken ever being taken seriously by the Commons on that subject again. But here we are, two and a half years later – a long time, but also not really a long time in a struggle as important as this – and the once unimaginable is now the norm.

The media turn round is welcome but it is also depressing. For it showed that after ten years of this government – ten years of lying on a scale never dreamed of before in this society in peace time – most of the managers of the higher media still relied upon the government and the state to tell it what was legitimate. One day Wallace is a fantasist, a professional liar and a murderer; Holroyd a paranoid nut-case. The next, they've got journalists running out of their ears – all because of a government statement.

It is now six years since the initial articles about Fred's experiences appeared in the *New Statesman*; ten years since the Kincora scandal was first broken by the *Irish Independent*. Yet the Channel Four News piece on Kincora a few weeks ago was the first substantial piece about it on British television.

This curious and lamentable state of affairs is not entirely, or perhaps even mostly, the fault of journalists. There are journalists who would be happy to chase the story down. Robert Parker at Channel Four News, for example, wanted to do just that in 1987. And there are others – not many, maybe, but some. But journalists, staff journalists, the ones in organisations with the resources to do such work, are not their own bosses. News editors set journalists' tasks; and they have other editors above them; and, ultimately there are owners and controllers.

Their reluctance to pursue this story – and this kind of story – is not easy to explain.

- It's partly about the cost of investigative journalism and the lack of a guaranteed 'product' at the end of the investigation.
- It's partly about the lack of public interest in this story – this is what is now grandly called 'news values', I think. The punters don't care, so it's not a story.
- It's partly about the lack of political interest – there is no clamour in the House of Commons. The Commons isn't interested, therefore it's not a story. In this respect the blame lies squarely on the Labour Party.
- It's also partly about the perceived dodgy status of Colin and Fred (which explains the great effort of the state to make them appear dodgy).

- And it's also about the reluctance of the higher media to risk the displeasure of the British state and the Conservative government. It has been the misfortune of Fred and Colin to have been trying to be heard during the Thatcher years. Not that it would have been easy under, say, James Callaghan – or Neil Kinnock. But it would have been *easier*.

This timidity is only partly explained by the fact that personnel in the higher reaches of the media actually support the Tory Party. That obviously does exist – the Mail, Telegraph, Times etc. It is also partly the result of the honours system. Media figures who please the Tory Party or the British state can now expect a gong. Sir Alastair Burnett; Sir Robin Day; Sir David Nicholas etc. The simple truth is – and here I am on Campaign for Press and Broadcasting Freedom territory – much of our media has been co-opted by the British state.

This goes back a long way. One starting point would be the Second World War when the media was largely controlled by the state. After the War, that state-media relationship was continued, especially overseas with the Information Research Department, the psy-war specialists, who turn up with Colin in Ireland. In the BBC, this state-media relationship was stunningly explicit. MI5 had an office in Broadcasting House – still does as far as I know. Alan Protheroe, until recently Assistant Director General of the BBC, was also a Territorial Army intelligence officer, specialising in Army-media relations. Newspapers have traditionally been used as cover by

MI6. Think of Philby at the *Observer*, David Holden at the *Sunday Times*. It is said that at one stage the entire foreign staff of the *Telegraph* was being subsidised by MI6. It is hardly surprising that the Iraqi government thought Mr Bazoft was a spy.[3] Last year John Le Carré – former intelligence officer David Cornwell – wrote of the early 1960s when 'most of the press was controlled by the intelligence services'. If that is true today, I can't see it. But the intelligence services have obvious assets in the *Sunday Telegraph*, *Sunday Express* and *Sunday Times*.

When Steve [Dorril] and I published our sketch of Colin's allegations, we headed our press release 'The British Watergate'. It seemed a decent analogy in 1986 and still is in as much as it conveys a sense of a great scandal and a cover-up. But it also conveys a misleading sense of the relative importance of the stories. Watergate was pretty small scale stuff compared to the Holroyd-Wallace story. Nobody got killed in Watergate, a few people went to jail; a few careers were ruined and one president was replaced by another, more or less the same. But the story of the British secret state's post-war operations and the state's involvement in Northern Ireland, is a much bigger stinking fish. In all its ramifications, this is the biggest domestic political story since World War 2. And it says something about our society and its political culture, that this meeting – the first to be organised with Fred and Colin since the story took off in February – should be happening in Manchester in front of a couple of dozen people. There is still no concerted parliamentary activity. There is still no official inquiry that I am aware of (though there must be a few commit-tees meeting in Whitehall to discuss how to contain this).

In the end, it is about power and accountability – the major themes of the Campaign for Press and Broad-casting Freedom. It's an old struggle. In the 50s there was a brief Campaign Against Secret Police Powers. 35 years later, here we are. The secret police have more powers, personnel and technology now than they had then. But we know a great deal more than our equivalents did in the mid 1950s and we aren't going away. The secrets are out now. We can just about piece together an outline of the British secret state's activities since the War. And though both Colin and Fred have gone to inordinate lengths not to blow the whistle on some of the things they know, we do owe them a lot in this regard. Just as the assassination of John Kennedy became a window through which the American secret state could be studied – the CIA, operations against Cuba, the FBI's Cointelpro operations, Vietnam – so the Holroyd-Wallace affair has provided the means to understand some of this state's secret history. Though they won't be comfortable in this role, when we do finally get a grip on the spooks in this country, we will owe them a lot.

Ireland is the great post-war crisis for the British state – 2000 civilian casualties; billions of pounds spent; many state employees, a minor member of the Royal Family, and the brains behind the then leader of the Tory Party, killed. Northern Ireland is the big one, the one they couldn't fix.

Colin worked in a small unit in Army HQ Northern Ireland, set up in 1971 to wage psychological warfare on Loyalist and Republican paramilitaries. It was staffed by the Army but trained by a seconded member of the Information Research Department (IRD). IRD was the British state's psy-war arm, and had been involved in most of the post-war colonial 'insurgencies', and was the last component of the standard, well-tried British state counterinsurgency armoury to be deployed in Northern Ireland: Army, MI6, MI5, IRD.

But IRD had grown up during the Cold War and could only play one tune – the Red Menace. They would find a communist connection to the IRA whether there was one or not. (And there basically wasn't.)

Evidence of IRD activities in the various colonial insurgencies is hard to find. But in Charles Foley's 1964 account of the war in Cyprus, *Legacy of Strife*, there is this paragraph:

'No effort was spared by the Secretariat to win over the foreign press with titillating stories. Sometimes, for the benefit of American correspondents, "captured documents" which they were not allowed to see, confirmed that EOKA was modelled on communist lines and that an increasing number of young communists were joining it. The official introduction of sex into the Cyprus problem was another product of this period. Reporters were invited to "Operation Tea-Party" in the Central News room and offered libations of everything but tea together with a handout declaring that schoolgirls had been "required to

prostitute themselves with fellow-members of EOKA". A later pamphlet described the sexual relations of such girls with members of the killer groups in one (unnamed) town, alleging that one of them had her first lover at the age of 12.'

IRD isn't named here but that is unmistakably IRD at work; and the same techniques were used in Ireland.

Yet, though the British state responded to the Northern Irish situation with the standard kit of counterinsurgency methods, this was not quite just another 'colonial war' as some on the Left would have us believe. No overall military/civil supremo was appointed as had been done in Malaya, for example, with Sir Gerald Templer; nor were the more extravagant techniques – mass deportation of populations, large-scale killings, collective punishments for communities supporting the insurgents – ever tried there. Previous insurgencies had not been dealt with under the noses of the world's media. In this 'insurgency', like no other in post-war British history, the presence of the media was a major inhibition.

Thanks largely to the insights provided by Fred and Colin, the strategies of the British state in Ireland between 1969 and 1975 are now visible in outline. After the Army was sent in, Edward Heath pushed MI6 into trying to sort things out and produce a quick solution. Under pressure, MI6 embarked on high-risk operations – such as using the Littlejohn brothers to play Bonnie and Clyde in 1972/3 in an attempt to discredit the Official IRA – and tried to arrange a peace deal with the Provos long before the ground had been prepared. (Gerry Adams was flown straight from internment to meet Willie Whitelaw.) Brigadier Frank Kitson, who had rewritten the Army's counterinsurgency manual in his 1970 *Low Intensity Operations*, was given command of a Brigade in Belfast to try out some of his ideas. Predictably, perhaps, this proved more difficult in Northern Ireland than it had in Africa, and several of his operations – MRF and the Four-Square Laundry come to mind – were blown.

MI6's attempts to do a deal with the IRA were unpopular with sections of the Army and exploited for bureaucratic ends by MI5. For MI5, Information Policy reprinted a Clann na hEireann pamphlet on the Littlejohn Affair, The Littlejohn Memorandum, to further embarrass MI6. The failure of the peace talks and the exposure of the Littlejohn operations enabled MI5 to mount a bureaucratic coup – the details of which are still unknown – and take over from MI6 as overall controllers of the intelligence war in Northern Ireland in 1974. More 'robust' methods became the order of the day and those who objected to the changes – Colin and Fred, for example – were got rid of.

It is clear in outline, if not yet in much detail, that mainland British politics in the '70s were seriously affected by the blow-back from the counterinsurgency operations in Northern Ireland. The Tory Party and the British state were captured by a hard-right Tory Party/military/intelligence alliance which first coalesced around policy in Northern Ireland. Between 1974 and 1979, Britain experienced a version of the 'strategy of tension' running in Italy. It is not a coincidence that the late Airey Neave should have been Mrs Thatcher's campaign manager, her spokesperson on Northern Ireland and the Shadow Cabinet member who approached Colin Wallace in 1976 for MI5's dirt on the Labour Party.

It is tempting to think of what happened here as a very British coup – 'very British' in that it was done fairly discreetly. No one now likes to mention it, and the hope is that if ignored, it will go away. But it is clear now that what happened between 1974 and 1979 was a very British *alternative* to a coup, the last stage before what one of the fringe participants described to me as 'the Chile option'.

Notes

1 Fred Holroyd and Colin Wallace were in the room, two of the other speakers that day. Fred Holroyd had been a Captain in the Special Military Intelligence Unit in Northern Ireland at the same time as Colin Wallace was serving as a press and psy-ops officer, though they had never worked together in the province. Holroyd had also worked for the MI6 officer in Northern Ireland, Craig Smellie, and, like Wallace, he had become a victim of the change in overall control of the British intelligence effort there when MI5 replaced MI6. Holroyd did not approve of some of the 'dirty tricks' being played by the British state and eventually blew the whistle in the *New Statesman*. He made contact with Wallace in Lewes prison and was working to get Wallace's manslaughter conviction overturned. Holroyd wrote a memoir, *War Without Honour*, which is now virtually unobtainable.

2 This refers to the announcement on January 30 1990 by the junior Defence Minister Archie Hamilton that there had indeed been a disinformation operation in Northern Ireland, in which Wallace had played a role. This was the first occasion on which the government had admitted this, provoking an explosion of media interest in Wallace.

3 Farzad Bazoft was a freelance journalist working for the *Observer* who was hanged as a spy in Iraq in 1990.

NEW LABOUR

CHAPTER FOURTEEN

The American Tendency and the Rise of New Labour

Talk to Islington Labour Party, 1996.

The Labour Party has been seized by a cabal. Blair, Brown and Mandleson have no more than 20 true believers in the PLP; estimates vary. Some put the figure of the Blairites as low as a dozen.

Gordon Brown used to tell interviewers that he spent his holidays in the library at Harvard University. In 1986, Tony Blair went on one of those US-sponsored trips to America that are available for promising MPs and came back a supporter of the nuclear deterrent. In 1993 he went to a meeting of the Bilderberg Group, one of the meeting places of the European-American elite at which promising young politicians are assessed for future promotion.

David Milliband, Blair's head of policy, did a Masters degree at MIT. Jonathan Powell, his foreign policy advisor, used to work in the British embassy in Washington and is said by some to have been the liaison officer between British intelligence and the CIA.

Ed Balls, Gordon Brown's economics advisor, 'studied at Harvard and was about to join the World

Bank' before he joined Brown. Sue Nye, Gordon Brown's personal assistant, is the partner of Gavyn Davies, economist with the predatory American bankers, Goldman Sachs.

And then there's Peter Mandleson. From his first year at Oxford, he was playing politics, first for the United Nations Association; and then, in his final year, 1976, as Chair of the British Youth Council. The British Youth Council used to be the British section of the World Assembly of Youth, which was set up and financed by MI6 and then taken over by the CIA in the 1950s. By Mandleson's time it was said to be financed by the Foreign Office, though that may be a euphemism for MI6.

In 1977, Mandleson and one Charles Clarke, then head of the British National Union of Students, put together a delegation from the UK to attend the 1978 World Festival of Youth, one of those Cold War jamborees crawling with spooks. Charles Clarke became Kinnock's chief gatekeeper at Walworth Road.

Mandleson, we were told in 1995 by Donald Mcintyre in *The Independent*, is 'a pillar of the two blue-chip foreign affairs think-tanks, Ditchley Park and Chatham House'.

The point I'm trying to make here is this: from their early twenties Clarke and Mandleson were already in the Whitehall system, young men on the make, players, albeit minor ones, in the Foreign Office game. (In something I wrote earlier on this subject I referred to them as 'premature careerists'.)

So, the Labour Party has been taken over by a little group whose orientation is overseas: the Foreign Office and its think tank satellites; Washington; America. Here is the source of the tension between so-called Old and New Labour. For who are the Labour Party's traditional constituencies? British domestic manufacturing; and British public sector workers. Old Labour is the domestic economy; New Labour is the overseas British economy. In other words the multinationals and the City.

But Tony Blair is just the latest manifestation of a tendency within the Labour Party, which runs with Hugh Gaitskell, through Roy Jenkins and the SDP, which has existed since the Cold War. They're the social democrats; and they should more properly be called the American Tendency.

The communism/anti-communism divide which is presented to us as the template of the post-war world masks the struggle between imperialism and nationalism. This is all familiar, I presume; the basic building blocks. Britain's position at the end of WW2 was paradoxical: on the one hand we were part of the winning team; on the other, we had sold off much of the family silver to pay for the War; and our partner, the USA, was determined to replace us as the world's leading imperial power.

In the late 1940s, the US began trying to supplant the older European empires – British, Dutch, French – with their own, informal empire. (They had already grabbed much of the old Spanish empire.) By an informal empire, I mean this: the Americans just wanted the doors open to their money and their goods. They weren't that interested in taking over the formal reins of power. Hence the reliance on the CIA and covert operations. Sort of clandestine imperialism. In Britain, the Conservatives were the party of the British empire and so the Americans were attracted to, and began to support, the anti-imperialist party – Labour. But the post-war Labour Party was left-ish; and, more important, a large chunk of it was economically nationalist and anti-imperialist. So the US funded and supported that section of the Labour Party which supported American internationalism – the social democrats; in effect the anti-socialist wing of the labour and trade union movements.

The requirements the US had of its clients in the post-war world varied with local conditions. For example the CIA funded – or ran – a wide spectrum of anti-communist but left-ish groups in the youth and student fields in the fifties and early 1960s. The World Assembly of Youth was one. In the remnants of the European colonial empires, the USA funded both nationalists and imperialists. In Algeria, for example, the Americans first funded some of the Algerian nationalists and then the OAS, the Secret Army Organisation of white colonialists. In the struggle with General de Gaulle, a French nationalist who opposed American expansion, the Americans showed most clearly that in politics there is only one important rule: my enemy's enemy is my friend.

Of the European social democrats, the US demanded support for the American post-war order: NATO, the

IMF, World Bank and GATT – what we now think of as the liberal capitalist order. The Americans supported the development of the EEC. The CIA funded the European Movement.

Part of that post-war international order was the international trade union movement. The British TUC joined in the US-run International Confederation of Free Trade Unions, the ICFTU, and its various spin-off groups, such as the trade secretariats, which were run – so it is claimed by CIA personnel – by the CIA. Whether the ICFTU and its network of organizations, are still run by the CIA, I don't know. The TUC helped fund the ICFTU through its affiliation fees. By the mid 1950s nearly a quarter of the TUC's annual budget was going to the ICFTU, a CIA operation.

US attempts to manipulate the British Labour Party and movement included the use of information officers and labour attaches in the Embassy in London. This climaxed with Joseph Godson, US labour attaché, whose career of tinkering with the British labour movement ran off and on from the fifties to the early 1980s. Godson got so close to the Gaitskellites that in the climactic struggle with the Bevanites, Gaitskell was planning strategy with Godson, running between Godson and the NEC.

Looking back now on a time when US personnel were producing magazines, funding factions, writing for journals etc. within the Labour Party and labour movement, it is difficult to imagine how this was tolerated. But part of the answer must be that the people the US State Department and CIA were using as their operatives in Europe, had all been on the US Left or in the union movement. To the gentlemen of the TUC in the '40s and '50s, Irving Brown, Jay Lovestone and Joseph Godson must have sounded just like them. They just didn't realise, I guess, that these American labour officials' first loyalty was to Uncle Sam and not to trade unionism.

The US, through the State Department and the Department of Labour, ran education programmes and freebie trips for sympathetic Labour movement people. Hundreds, maybe thousands – no-one has yet assembled the data – of British trade union officials and MPs had these freebies.

The relationships between individual British unions and the USA has not been researched, but there are little fragments in the literature which show some unions to have been more enthusiastic about the American connection than others. What is now the GMB and the old Post Office Workers union, in particular, were very close to US interests at one point. We know almost nothing about this and the research now may never get done – because many of the people concerned are dead.

The CIA ran the Congress for Cultural Freedom which published magazines all over Europe and organised big conferences to which the British social democrat leaders were invited, and for whom Anthony Crosland worked. In Britain, through the columns of *Encounter* magazine, this network promoted the Gaitskellites.

The CIA also funded and ran the international youth and student movements in the West; the Soviets funded rival groups.

In other words, much of the international political landscape of the post-war era consisted of US-funded or directed political projects; and this on top of the military-diplomatic-financial structure of NATO, IMF etc. At one level this is banal: in the American-dominated world, to get along you went along with the Americans.

So far, I have been describing what might best be called psychological warfare programs. But there were also the intelligence gathering and policing functions. The State Department, via the London embassy, was sending back masses of reports. None of these British reports have surfaced but over 1000 pages of such reports made by the New Zealand US embassy to the State Department on the tiny NZ labour movement have been declassified and show surveillance down to the level of trades councils and union branches. It seems a reasonable assumption that the same attention to detail was being exercised on the strategically far more significant British labour movement.

Under the anti-communist banner, a series of domestic anti-left groups were, I believe, funded by the CIA in Britain. Let me emphasise *believe*; for I have little concrete evidence. This network begins with Common Cause, which then produced an offshoot, Industrial Research and Information Services, IRIS, in the mid 1950s to work in the unions. Common Cause and IRIS produced information and propaganda against what it called 'communists', and IRIS set up 'cells' – its word – in unions to combat the Left. The significance of this is impossible to evaluate; the man who was running IRIS for much of this period won't answer my questions and what was left of Common Cause claimed, in 1987, to have no records.

Another clandestine strand begins with the psychological warfare organisation IRD, the Information Research Department. Set up within the Foreign Office in 1948, IRD worked abroad trying to combat nationalism in the British Empire, and at home to combat the British Left. IRD fed information into the Labour Party bureaucracy on 'communists' within the movement; into the unions through a list of confidential recipients of its briefings – one of whom we now know was the late Vic Feather – and directly into the Labour Party's policing units, the National Agent's Department and the Organisation Subcommittee. These latter organisations also received information on a local basis from police Special Branches. Again, this was all done under the banner of anti-communism.

So, if we freeze things at 1963, just before the death of Hugh Gaitskell, the situation in the Labour Party was this: it was being surveilled by Special Branches, the US State Department, and the Foreign Office's IRD. Information and disinformation on the Left was being collected and distributed by Common Cause and IRIS – run in my opinion, by the CIA – and by IRD through its network of journalists, union leaders and politicians. All of this information, where pertinent, was being fed into the Labour Party's organisation via the National Agent's Department and the Organisation Subcommittee – the latter, in 1963, chaired by George Brown, one of the CIA's sources in the Party.

The Gaitskellites had a pretty complete grip on the party; their leaders were being boosted, legitimised and discretely subsidised by the CIA through the Congress for Cultural Freedom; and their trade union allies in the major unions had everything under control having seen off the Left's challenge over unilateralism. Unfortunately Hugh Gaitskell died, the Labour Right couldn't decide on a single candidate, and the leadership election was won by Harold Wilson, who had never been part of this network; who had spent the Cold War travelling to Moscow, not to Washington.

This is a quick skim across a lot of very complicated material, some of which is described in more detail in the pamphlet I wrote and published earlier this year, *The Clandestine Caucus*.

The Wilson years have been researched in more detail and we can skim across them even more quickly. MI5, encouraged by a section of the CIA, began ploughing through the PLP and Wilson's entourage looking for Soviet espionage. (And found none, incidentally.)

In my opinion, the leadership of the American tendency passed to Roy Jenkins and its focus shifted to the Common Market. Members of the American tendency plotted constantly against Wilson. In 1967 the CIA's funding of the National Students Association in America was revealed and, quite quickly the whole network of fronts began to unravel.

The revelation of its Cold War fronts persuaded the CIA that its future lay in more discrete operations with better cover. Lots of apparently independent think tanks began to appear on the scene. Brian Crozier's Institute for the Study of Conflict was a pioneer in this field.

The old networks continued but with less effect. In the mid-1970s, Common Cause funded the Trade Union Centre for Education in Democratic Socialism in London; and in the 1980s the same people seem to me to have been involved in the formation of the group Mainstream. The activities of the network, Common Cause, IRIS, through to Mainstream in the 1980s, were centred round two unions, the engineers and electricians; and this activity came to a kind of appropriate resolution recently when Bill Jordan, of the EEEPTU, the amalgamation of the engineers and electricians, who was the nominal head of Mainstream, became President of the ICFTU, which had been the CIA's labour front of the 1950s. (There is no evidence that Bill Jordan had any links to the CIA.)

When Labour won the election in February 1974, IRD abandoned its briefings on the domestic left for fear of political embarrassment and that role was picked up by Brian Crozier, who had been working with IRD and the CIA, as he tells us in his memoirs, since the 1950s. In the 1970s, Crozier created what were essentially private sector versions of IRD's intelligence gathering and clandestine briefings on the British Left, and the CIA's covert political actions. He had some input into the Social Democratic Alliance in the mid 1970s, the forerunner of the SDP, briefed Mrs Thatcher, while she was leader of the opposition, on the 'communist menace', and began producing IRD-type briefings on the British Left. These were published by . . . IRIS.

On top of – or below – all this, MI5 surveilled the British Left; penetrated everything from CND through to INLA; investigated and/or smeared and/or blackmailed dozens of Labour MPs (and Tory and Liberal MPs), and, most importantly, it now seems to me, helped keep the Communist Party of Great Britain (CPGB) going.

Through the unions and through dialogue with some of the Labour Left, the CPGB did have some influence on the Labour Party, in particular in the 1970s. On this the Right is correct. How much influence they had – opinions vary. But the fact that they had any influence at all is largely down to MI5. The CPGB's big problem was the Soviet Union, and though it later strove to present itself as independent of the Soviets, the presumed link did it terrible damage as the nature of the Soviet regime was revealed in the 1950s, notably in Hungary, when about a third of the membership – including my parents – quit the Party. And we now know there really was Soviet gold in the CPGB; sacks of used notes were transferred from the Soviet Embassy to King St. But the point is this: *MI5 knew about this as soon as it started*. Peter Wright told us in *Spycatcher*, several years before messrs Falber and Matthews of the CPGB Central Committee at the time confessed. And MI5 chose to let the money continue. At any time after 1957, MI5 could have exposed the Soviet funding of the CPGB. Had they done so in, say, 1959, in what state would the CPGB have been in the 1960s?

Even in the midst of the big flap after the 1973 abolition of the Labour Party's proscription list,[1] which MI5 and its allies presented as opening the floodgates to

Soviet penetration, they keep the Soviet funding secret. With private armies forming in the Home Counties, the British Army doing manoeuvres at Heathrow and *The Times* discussing the conditions for a British military coup – even then, when, had you believed the *Daily Telegraph*, the state itself was under threat from militant unions run by the Communist Party, even then MI5 chose not to reveal the Soviet funding of the CPGB.

In effect MI5 ran the CPGB as a honey-trap for the Labour movement.

The alliances of intelligence, military and financial circles which had run the disinformation campaigns against the Labour government in the 1970s, helped elect Mrs Thatcher leader of the Tory Party and then as Prime Minister. Mrs T, contrary to popular belief, wasn't very bright, and while professing to want to rebuild the British domestic economy, actually turned the City of London loose, abolished exchange controls, and wrecked the domestic economy. The City and the overseas sector boomed, while the domestic economy crumbled. The basic fault line in British society was never more nakedly exposed. The President of the CBI spoke of a 'bare knuckle fight' with the Tory government. (He was sacked almost immediately afterwards.)

The City versus industry conflict *was* recognised in some sections of the Labour Party, notably by Bryan Gould, and the Labour Party began producing policies to deal with it. But in 1986 Neil Kinnock *et al* decided to support Britain's membership of the EEC and from that point the game was up. For EEC membership was incompatible with the kinds of nationalist, anti-free trade policies being produced by the committee chaired by Bryan Gould. So Gould got dumped and the leadership of the PLP began the process of making itself respectable to the moneylenders. After 1992, John Smith, Gordon Brown and Mo Mowlam embarked on the so-called 'prawn cocktail offensive' – eating their way round the City's executive dining rooms, promising not to do anything to restrict their activities. (Mo Mowlam subsequently married a banker.) This grovelling before the moneylenders climaxed with Labour's support for membership of the Exchange Rate Mechanism, which, Bryan Gould reports in his memoir, Gordon Brown sold to the PLP as a socialist measure to nobble the speculators!

And so we reach the present day. It is worth remembering that the important moves were made by Kinnock and Smith. Tony Blair is merely putting the gloss on; dumping the remnants of the ideological baggage, emasculating the membership and the unions, prior to instituting state funding of the political parties and the final transformation of the Labour Party into the reliable political face of the European Union, NATO, the global economy and the power of the moneylenders.

Notes

1 The proscription list consisted of political groups, membership of which was incompatible with membership of the Labour Party. They were fronts of the Communist Party of Great Britain or the Trostskyist groups and parties. Abolishing the list meant it was possible for members of the Militant Tendency, for example, to infiltrate the Labour Party and, as in Liverpool in the early 1980s, take over the local party.

CHAPTER FIFTEEN

New Labour and the City

Talk given in 1998 to the Avenues branch of Hull North Labour Party – the branch of which I had been Secretary in the early 1990s.

The *Prawn Cocktail Party* is my second book about the Labour Party. When the first one, *Smear! Wilson and the Secret State*, came out in 1991, when I was still active in the Party, I didn't get invited to talk to a single branch in Hull – not even this one. So, I thought, this time I'm going to invite myself .

I'm not here to plug my book. The publisher made a mess of it; did the whole thing in a hurry to meet some deadline; and like most things done in a hurry, it's a mess. In a hurry, the publisher skipped the stage where the author gets a proof copy of the text to read to check for mistakes. As a result the publisher has scrambled the footnotes to three of the chapters and added various other errors. I wanted the entire print-run pulped and redone. If, at the end of this, anyone wants to read in more detail about what I am saying, the most important chapter of the book, as far as the Blair faction goes, has been published in a magazine published in Scotland, *Variant* – and I have some free copies. Just take one before you leave. [It is reproduced in the Appendix at the end of this book.]

I'm going to present essentially a polemical cartoon: in 20 minutes, which is what I was asked to do, I can do little else.

We are members of a party which has been taken over by a little clique. There are obvious analogies with the middle-of-the-road Tories after Thatcher seized the Tory Party and won the '79 election. The analogy is closer than you might think, for between 1979 and 1982 the Tories jacked-up interest rates, maintaining an uncompetitive pound, just as Gordon Brown has done since Labour won in 1997. The Tories destroyed a quarter of the British manufacturing base – while protesting that it was beyond their control. Gordon Brown looks set fair to destroy some more of what's left of the manufacturing base in the recession which is just beginning – while, like the Thatcher government, protesting it's beyond his control. In 1981-2 the Tories blamed North Sea oil for pushing up the value of the pound. Gordon Brown doesn't have North Sea oil revenues to blame, he blames the world economy; and he blames British manufacturing for not being able to live with an overvalued pound – just as Mrs Thatcher did. Like the Tory Thatcherites, New Labour blames the victim.

The analogies with the Thatcher years are closer yet. Mrs Thatcher and her first Chancellor of the Exchequer, Geoffrey Howe, knew nothing about economics and implemented an agenda prepared for them by the City of London. Tony Blair and Gordon Brown know nothing about economics and have done exactly the same thing – and for the same people.

In economics, we have a Thatcherite government in office. In most of the social policy areas, there is little difference. Thatcher and co. believed in private education (subsidised by the state); private medicine (subsidised by the state); private pensions; privatisation; and the free play of market forces. The Blairites believe the same.

Nor is this being kept a secret: Tony Blair actually said at this year's conference, 'there is no alternative' – Mrs Thatcher's famous and fatuous confession of economic ignorance. Gordon Brown at this year's conference echoed her famous 'U-turn if you want to, the lady's not for turning' speech. These are quite deliberate echoing of Mrs Thatcher – an expression of utter contempt for the party members who don't share their admiration for the Iron Lady.

How did this happen? Usually, historical and political changes are difficult to trace but in this instance there are a number of clear decisions which took us here.

The first was the decision by Neil Kinnock to support membership of the EEC as it then was. Mostly this decision was made because Thatcher was increasingly against the EEC. If she was agin it, we had to be for it. Having made this decision, everything else then slotted into place. Becoming pro-EEC meant abandoning most of the existing Labour Party economic policy which was focused on rebuilding manufacturing and controlling the financial sector. Kinnock wrote a book, *Making Our Way*, expressing these views – and doing it rather well, in fact – which, ironically, was published only a few months before he changed his mind.

After the 1987 election defeat, John Smith was Shadow Chancellor. Knowing nothing about economics, he pulled together a group of advisors. By 1988 he, his advisors and Kinnock, had decided that Labour should support Britain's membership of the Exchange Rate Mechanism, the ERM. Being pro-ERM and pro-EEC meant, in effect, surrendering much of Britain's economic policy to Brussels. Having concluded this, Smith decided to go the whole hog and give up any idea of controlling the financial sector. So began the 'prawn cocktail offensive', the process in which Smith, Brown and Marjorie Molam toured the City of London reassuring the bankers that Labour, if elected, would do nothing to restrict their activities or threaten their profits. This wasn't enough to get Labour elected in 1992; but just after the election we had the ERM fiasco, when the pound was finally forced out of the ERM, destroying the centrepiece of the Tory government's economic policy. This is where the Tories lost the 1997 election: they were seen to be incompetent. Nobody seemed to notice that the Labour opposition also supported this insane policy.

Labour wooed the City - not the domestic economy, not the manufacturing economy. In 1989, having decided that Labour had to become the wholehearted party of capitalism, Mowlam and Smith went to the City of London, not to the CBI or the regional Chambers of Commerce. After 1992 Labour set out to be the party of the financial sector. Labour promised to be a more reliable bet for continued membership of the EEC, which the City wanted, and thus a more reliable guarantor of City profits than the Tories. For, unlike Labour, the Tories had a sizeable wing hostile to British membership of the EEC. If the City supported the Tories they might end up with a nationalist Tory Party in office bent on withdrawing from the EEC/EU. So the City (and thus the media) supported Blair and Brown who promised in the years leading up to the 1997 election, to stay in Europe, to look after the City's interests; to keep public spending down; to be 'prudent' – which is code for keeping interest rates (and thus the value of the pound) high.

It is worth restating this: everything flowed from the decision to support membership of the EEC and then to support ERM membership. Blame Kinnock and Smith.

Along with this return to economic (i.e. City) economic orthodoxy, Labour's defence policy reverted to the old gang of pro-Americans gathered round the Trade Union Committee for European and Transatlantic Understanding – TUCETU for short – created by one Joseph Godson. This is worth following here for continuity. [See also previous chapter.]

From 1956–1959, Joseph Godson was the US labour attaché, working with Hugh Gaitskell against the Labour Left led by Bevan. (There had been a decade of US intervention in the Labour Party and trade unions after WW2, to stop it going left.) In the 1970s, Godson, formally retired, returned to Britain and formed the Labour Committee on Transatlantic Understanding (LCTU), a CIA front, which took rising young Labour MPs and trade unionists off to the States and showed them: (a) a good time and (b) that if they wanted to prosper, the thing to do is get on the team. Go along to get along. In the 1980s, the Labour Committee on Transatlantic Understanding, added Europe to its name, incorporated Peace Through NATO, the anti-CND group, and began getting funding from the British Foreign Office. It has always been US policy to have Britain in the EEC/EU, as their proxy – and lo and behold, when Labour returned to office in 1997, the entire Labour defence team had come from this Committee and its partner, the Atlantic Council.

30 years later Joe Godson's little operation is still paying off. (His son, Dean Godson, is currently writing for the *Daily Telegraph*.)

[At this point I read a section from the material reproduced in the Appendix at the end of this talk.]

Modernisation means maintaining the City's hegemony – high interest rates; no controls on capital; no increases in income tax for the rich; no redistribution; supporting the US. The Bill and Tony show succeeds the Bill and John show; which succeeds the Margaret and Ronnie show.

This has the usual consequences: declining manufacturing; increasing polarisation between London and the rest of the country; between the rich and the not rich.

It is all predictable – and predicted.

Now we have a crisis: a recession has been created by the overvalued pound – just as in 1980-83. Everything Brown and Blair believed since 1988/9 is turning out to be false. But will they change their minds? No they won't. Public spending will be cut. Tough luck on the disabled, the public sector, immigrants, refugees, single parents – all the usual scapegoats.

And we're stuck. The Blairites have taken control of the party's conference, the policy-making machinery, and candidate selection with an efficiency which must make the Militant Tendency as was green with envy. If you're not with the ticket you don't get on the bus. We are utterly powerless.

Comment

My talk was not believed by many of those present. The picture I was presenting of the New Labour faction's take-over of the party, and the consequences, was too difficult to take on board. The usual defence mechanism – denial – was still strong in those days. But since then, along with almost all the members of that branch, I have resigned from the Labour Party. The Avenues branch which used to have between 20 and 30 present at routine monthly meetings, now has meetings of 3 or 4 – if it meets at all.

CHAPTER SIXTEEN

The Anglo-American Special Relationship and the British American Project (BAP)

Talk to the Islington Labour Party, House of Commons, 1999.

I have to start by going through the ritual of denying that I am anti-American. I grew up saturated in US culture: jazz, Voice of America on my trannie; R and B, blues; I can vividly remember the trad boom, the r and b boom; the American novel, movies, paintings – the beats – Kerouac, Mailer, James Baldwin, Blue Note record sleeves – these left indelible marks on my tastes. All that cultural imperialism in the 1950s paid off with me. Virtually without exception the Americans I have met I have liked: for the most part the clichés about them being open, friendly, and generous are all true. But the average Americans who are such delightful people to drink beer with, have no knowledge of and no role in, US foreign policy. And it is US foreign policy which I oppose.

The story is terribly simple at this distance. The US supplanted the British as the leading world power at the end of WW2. School had a new bully. Instead of opposing US power, as the French did, our state and most of our politicians decided to go along to get along. The US official Dean Acheson famously said some years after the Suez debacle, when the US reminded the British state who was the dominant partner, that Britain had lost an empire but not found a role. Acheson's epigram is always quoted with approval but is, in fact, entirely wrong. By the time he said it, Britain had already adopted the role of the new school bully's best friend – a role it is still playing; doing what the school bully's best friend does: grovelling obedience when he's around; bitching and name-calling when he's not.

Since Suez, the only fundamental thing that has changed is the constant decline of the military forces the UK has to bring to the party, and the shrinking areas of the world in which UK power is greater than that of the US. Something under 5% of the Anglo-American force which attacked Iraq in Operation Desert Storm was British. Britain's contribution to the Special Relationship is basically now down to that of symbolic evidence of 'international support'. That Tony Blair *et al* dress this up with the rhetoric of morality deserves our derision – or our pity for their delusions. Britain really is, as Pat Buchanan put it recently, the mouse that roars.

But the US did not – and does not – take this support for granted. It was created and is maintained. After WW2, the US set about buying or coercing all possible opposition groups. In Europe, first, and eventually in virtually the entire non-communist world, right down to tiny New Zealand where Freedom of Information documents show that in the 1950s the US was surveilling the entire New Zealand labour movement right down to union branch level.

It was done with carrots and sticks, the traditional tools. But where Britain was concerned, mostly it was done with carrots. The carrots were money, freebies, trips, education, courses and holidays in the US; sometimes simply bribes or jobs; and an increased likelihood of promotion for members of the US-supported team.

One of the saddest things about this is how little it took to buy the British labour movement. Just as John Poulson was able to buy planning committee decisions in Labour councils in the 1960s and '70s for a holiday in Spain for key members of the committees, the US seems to have bought large sections of the British labour movement for little more.

By the late 1950s, all the non-communist bloc transnational union bodies were run by the US, many by the CIA. Journalists got and still get what is known as the 'CIA tour' – a couple of days of meetings, lectures and visits, followed by a fortnight's free travel in the US. Formal programmes to pay the way for sympathetic Brits have included Harkness, Fulbright, Kennedy scholarships; various Congressional programs, the Smith-Mundt scholarships, Eisenhower Exchange Fellowships, and the State Department's Young Leader programme (which embraced Roy Hattersley and Margaret Thatcher). In 1983, one of the first things newly elected MP Tony Blair did was take the American freebie trip.

At another level, there are all the various transatlantic forums at which the US and UK elite meet, get to know each other and come to a consensus about the issues of the day – which, oddly enough, almost invariably coincides with the US agenda. These are the: Ditchley Foundation, Royal Institute for International Affairs, Bilderberg conferences, and Trilateral Commission. Bilderberg is the one of current interest to me because I was recently informed by Bilderberg's administrator that the late John Smith was on the Bilderberg Steering Group from 1989 to 1992. Those of you still clinging to the notion that Smith was some kind of hero of old Labour, please note.

And then there are those groups allied to and or funded by NATO: the British Atlantic Committee, the Atlantic Council, the British North-American Committee, the British Atlantic Group of Young Politicians (now defunct, I think), the Trade Union Committee for European and Transatlantic Understanding, Atlantic Education Trust, Atlantic Information Centre for Teachers, the Standing Conference of Atlantic Organisations and who knows what others you would find if you had a systematic hunt. As a basic rule of thumb, there will always be money available to members of left parties who support US policies.

The immediate cause of my invitation this evening was an article I published just after the 1997 election on the latest of these Anglo-American groups, The British American Project for the Future Generation, now just known as the British American Project, or BAP for short. Since I published Tom Easton's piece on the BAP in *Lobster*, the Easton material has been reworked by John Pilger and Paul Foot, and this attention has provoked the

BAP to produce a pamphlet describing its origins. The pamphlet is very interesting indeed, though perhaps not for the reasons the author intended.

Nick Butler, we are told in the BAP pamphlet, 'originally thought of the Project as a way of putting Labour people like himself in touch with American ideas – but on economic and social issues.'

This is a fairy story, of course. It was 1982 – before Tony Blair had been elected as an MP. Butler was already part of the Atlanticist network as a 27 year-old Research Fellow at the Royal Institute for International Affairs (as well as an economist with BP) and had his feet on the rungs of promotion within the Labour Party as Treasurer of the Fabian Society. In 1982 the UK was in the depths of the Thatcher/Lawson/Howe-created depression;

- the Tories were showing the lowest poll ratings since polls had been created;
- CND was booming;
- anti-nuclear (and thus anti-American) campaigns were blossoming all over Western Europe.

It is this context, rather than Butler's professed desire to learn about US thinking on economic and social issues, which inspired Butler to write a memo to David Watt, then director of the RIIA, in which he said: 'We start from the point of view that as well as the active hostility to all things American from some parts of the political spectrum here, there is in addition a serious lack of mutual understanding over a wide range of policies';

220

and he mooted 'the possibility of establishing some form of regular contact for Britons and Americans similar in style and purpose to Konigswinter.'

Konigswinter is the Foreign Office-sponsored forum where Brits and Germans have met since the end of WW2, much frequented by the remnants of the Gaitskellite wing of the Labour Party in the '60s and '70s who turned into the SDP.

In other words, in 1982 the Anglo-American political alliance looked in danger; there was a chance that the Conservative Party would lose the next General Election (the Falklands card had not then been played) and something had to be done. And unlike CND which raised its own money as far as I know, young Mr Butler, we are told, got $1000 from the US embassy in London to take a couple of chums across to the States to beat the bushes for private sector funding for his project. Which private funding was duly forthcoming to the tune of some hundreds of thousands of pounds and off the jamboree set. And, presumably because it was initiated by a member of the Labour Party, a large number of people now associated with New Labour have been among those invited to the BAP bean-feasts.

After the 1997 election, the BAP newsletter headline was 'Big Swing to BAP' as it celebrated the arrival of 5 BAP alumni in the Labour government: namely Marjorie Mowlam, Chris Smith, Peter Mandelson, George Robertson and Elizabeth Symons. Also recipients of the BAP bounty have been Jonathan Powell, Blair's chief of staff, and Geoff Mulgan, via Militant and Red Wedge, now in the Downing Street Policy Unit, and Matthew Taylor, Head of Policy at Millbank at one time, as well as various MPs.

The BAP is interesting but neither exceptional nor probably terribly influential. These groups are not about conspiratorial manipulation of policy. The US hardly needs to manipulate policy so long as it can continue to persuade the British political classes to maintain the Atlanticist consensus. Groups like the BAP are about maintaining the group think, the kind of instinctive pro-American, pro-NATO consensus which is so powerful in this country, that as soon as you stray from it, Jeremy Paxman's eyebrow rises and his voice gives the viewers the cue that, yes, this person isn't to be taken seriously. (Paxman has been on BAP jamborees.)

The British state was constructed to run an empire. The buildings which house it are all over central London. And, alas – absurdly, preposterously – the attitudes of empire are still there, too. At the heart of these attitudes is the notion of Britain as a great power, a world power with 'responsibilities' – a power based on the international role of British capital. Along with the empire – more or less defunct – goes the ancient role of the City of London as financial centre to the world.

This imperial system is still – absurdly, preposterously – insulated from political accountability. Foreign policy, defence, the intelligence and security services, and the police which keep the domestic population in line, these are off the political agenda; specifically not accountable to parliament; or, if you like, to the will of the people.

New Labour's distinctive contribution to this was to add control of interest rates to the list of areas beyond the reach of the peoples' representatives – thus giving the Bank of England something it had sought since 1945.

And if this sounds like the old Bennite agenda, it is in a way; but it was also the agenda of the Union for Democratic Control which was formed during WW1.

The central problem in Britain is the state and what is now called the core institutional nexus of the Treasury-City and Bank of England. When Eddie George was inept enough to acknowledge some months ago that unemployment in the North of England was a price worth paying for 'defeating inflation' he was merely articulating one of the base assumptions of the overseas lobby: the domestic economy is always sacrificed to the interests of the overseas one. If Eddie George was a stick of rock this would be part of the writing running through him. Eddie George can dismiss the fate of manufacturing in the North of England because the Treasury and Bank of England decided to abandon manufacturing in the late 1970s when the scale of North Sea oil revenues became apparent. Hence all the talk about the post-industrial society during the Thatcher governments.

Since Britain no longer has the military or diplomatic clout to protect its overseas investments, it has to use the Americans. Hence the Bill and Tony show, which was preceded by the Bill and John Major show and before that the Margaret and George Bush show and the Margaret and Ronnie show. Hence, still, the Visiting

Forces Act of 1952, which makes US personnel in their various bases in the UK exempt from British law.

It is our misfortune to be members of a party which has been seized by a small group of what we might call naive fans of America. This group is convinced that, despite the US being a mineral-rich, underpopulated continent consuming about two fifths of the world's resources, it is a good model for this tiny, overcrowded island.

This is an extremely strange phenomenon – as odd as the infatuation some of the British Left had with Stalin's Soviet Union in the 1930s. Looking to the US for its military power, this makes a kind of sense. But looking to the US for economic or domestic policies is dotty in the extreme. Urban America is a violent, brutal, extremely mobile society. A quarter of the American population move house and job every year; and every year 25,000 of them are shot to death.

Britain has far more in common with, say, Denmark, than it does with the US. But reality has nothing to do with it.

How we escape this I don't know. At some point, maybe quite soon, the US trade deficit will become unsustainable and the US treasury will put up interest rates to persuade the rest of the world to continue buying its public debt. UK interest rates will rise. They are already twice what they are in the Euro zone – which is why the pound is so high and British exporters are continuing to go down the pan. US interest rate rises will push UK interest rates up and the pound even higher.

What's left of UK manufacturing will crumble some more and unemployment will rise. Somewhere, in all this, we are supposed to be entering the single currency. If we do, we will enter at too high a rate for sterling. Just as we returned to the Gold Standard too high in 1926. Just as we entered the ERM too high in 1989. And the same consequences will occur: more unemployment and more manufacturing losses. But this doesn't matter to the core institutional nexus in London: they wrote manufacturing off over 20 years ago.

New Labour's leaders think they have moved beyond ideology. I have heard Tony Blair use that expression. New Labour's leaders are too young and too ill-informed to recognise that the expression 'Beyond ideology' was coined in the great 1950s CIA psy-war operations. They are also too dim to grasp that professing no ideology is an ideology in itself, as much now as it was in the 1950s when the CIA was paying the Gaitskellites, the present lot's predecessors, to jet round the world on jamborees for the Congress for Cultural Freedom.

Having spent most of their lives pursuing their careers, Tony Blair, and the little cabal around him, are rather ignorant of history as well as not being very bright – at least not by the standards of, say, the Wilson cabinet. They are also true believers in The Future with a capital F, Technology with a capital T, Science with a Capital S and Progress with a capital P.

As we approach the beginning of the final year of the Millennium – and it is somehow entirely appropriate that the great Millennium celebrations are being held a year too early – our party is being led by a bunch of naive modernists who haven't grasped that the things they value are going to destroy the planet.

What can we do about all this . . . well don't resign, first; and don't believe the hype, second; and trust your own judgement, third. If Tony Blair looks like a rather prissy public schoolboy who has had virtually no experience of the real world, it's because that's what he actually is. If the party appears to be in the grip of a group of Stalinist careerists, it's because it is. All we can do for the moment is wait for economic realities to impinge and keep alive the older, more rational, and better informed intellectual traditions which this party still contains.

Oh yes, and join Labour Reform.

CHAPTER SEVENTEEN

The Origins of New Labour

Talk to Labour Reform Conference, London, 2002.

We have to go back at least as far as the 1980s. The book I wrote on this subject begins with Edward Heath . . .

In 1985 Labour was anti-nuclear (i.e. anti-American), anti-EEC and anti-the City. And trying to rid itself of the Militant Tendency. The election loss in 1987 confirmed what the leadership of the party believed: its policies – those policies in particular – were preventing it from gaining power. Kinnock and Hattersley began the policy review – essentially a cover story for ditching its central policies on the economy, the link with the United States and EEC membership.

The opposition to the EEC was abandoned: the EEC ceased to be a capitalist club and became a socialist – or statist – bulwark; Jacques Delors came to the TUC and told them the EEC would protect unions against Mrs Thatcher.

Opposition to nukes was abandoned.

And economic policy was changed after Bryan Gould, who had chaired the policy review group on the economy, was moved to shadow environment. John Smith became Shadow Chancellor with Gordon Brown his deputy. Smith toured the City with Mo Mowlam, assuring the bankers that in office Labour would do nothing to reduce their freedom or their profits. International currency dealers were promised there would be no attempt to bring back exchange controls; a group of bankers were assured that Labour did not intend to nationalise the banks – something which the party had not seriously considered in the previous fifty years!

This 'prawn cocktail offensive', as it became derisively known, was the most complete and protracted act of political surrender in British history. Neil Lawson, former aid to Gordon Brown, said of this period: 'Labour got to the stage in the early 1990s where we'd give up virtually anything to get elected'.

By 1992 they *had* given up virtually everything.

All of this is before Blair.

We got roses and smart suits and Labour Listens; Kinnock got a haircut and we got Peter Mandelson's early attempts to gild the lily. And Labour lost again in '92.

Kinnock quit and was rewarded for bringing Labour into the EEC fold with a commissioner's job in Brussels.

John Smith was challenged for the leadership by Bryan Gould. Gould was the last major Labour figure at that time to oppose the EEC and the City. Smith won and Gould left UK politics for New Zealand.

All of this will be familiar – or maybe vaguely familiar. But here's the first bit which might not be. When John Smith became leader of the Labour Party he was a member of the steering committee of the Bilderberg

Group; the steering committee, the inner core. He got Gordon Brown invited to the 1991 meeting, incidentally. At Bilderberg, politicians meet the leaders of the big companies on the q.t.. Globalisation is the taken-for-granted agenda.

Who *was* John Smith? Genial, whiskey-drinking Scots lawyer from the traditional Labour Right. But also life-long chums with a senior MI6 officer, now Baroness Ramsay. Lady Smith, his widow, is now on the board of a company formed by senior MI6 people. And there's his Bilderberg role. Bilderberg: the leading European-American forum for globalisation.

Under Smith, Gordon Brown became Shadow Chancellor. Brown was a traditional Labour figure: the economic spokesman who doesn't know much about economics. He took on an advisor – Ed Balls, a *Financial Times* leader writer; an ideologist for globalisation, in effect – who learned some of his economics at Harvard. Like other Labour personnel, including Yvette Cooper MP, whom Balls later married, and David Miliband, head of Blair's policy unit, both now junior ministers, Balls had spent a year in America as a Kennedy Scholar.

Virtually all of the New Labour people have some connection to America and American money.

Ed Balls took Gordon to America and introduced him – the probable next Chancellor of the Exchequer – to the people he met at Harvard. Brown starts going to New England for his summer holidays and gets the neo-liberal line from the Harvard profs: globalisation, the Washington consensus.

Brown and Tony Blair start getting the attention of the media. The coming men. And true believers in the American way. By 1988 Labour leader Neil Kinnock, John Smith and Gordon Brown (and their advisers) had concluded that Labour should advocate British membership of the European Exchange Rate Mechanism (ERM) as the first step towards an eventual single European currency. But they decided to become advocates of ERM membership not for economic reasons, but because it was perceived by them to be a way of demonstrating to the City that they were trustworthy; ERM membership would be a guarantee there would be no more attempts to run an independent economic policy. For most of Labour's leaders had concluded that the City of London was too powerful to challenge. *This is the origins of New Labour*.

After Black Wednesday in 1992, when the pound was forced out of the exchange rate mechanism, after the Tories' second big recession, the political system knew that the Tories would lose the next election: their economic incompetence had finally been rumbled. John Smith would wait; he believed oppositions didn't win elections; governments lost them.

Tony Blair took the US government's free tour of the States in '86 and told his hosts that while officially a member of CND he supported the nuclear deterrent. He had joined the Labour Friends of Israel in 1983 when he got elected. While Shadow Home Secretary in 1994, Tony Blair took an Israeli government freebie holiday in Israel. On his return the number two at the Israeli embassy in

London introduced him to Michael Levy – now Lord Levy – one of the top fund-raisers for Jewish charities. Blair and Levy hit it off.

Blair and Brown, the rising stars, who want to get on with 'modernising' things, are impatient with John Smith's caution; but Smith died before the splits appeared and Blair succeeded him. Michael Levy then raised some millions – £7 million is the figure widely quoted – for Tony Blair's private office. And thus the Labour Party lost whatever little hold it had on its leader: Blair didn't need the party's money. And the Israeli lobby in the UK got a very pro-Israeli prime minister.

Blair assembled the team: Mandelson, Phillip Gould, Jonathan Powell from the British embassy in Washington, and Alastair Campbell. They visited America and copied the Democrats' policies, slogans and campaign style.

Brown, Blair, Powell, Campbell, Gould, and Mandelson, made up virtually the whole of 'New Labour'. Powell seems the least significant, a technician who came aboard long after the ship had sailed. Campbell has become a very significant player and was sometimes referred to as 'the real deputy prime minister' during Blair's first term. (The portrait of him and Blair in the Rory Bremner Show on Channel 4, with Campbell bossing Blair, is apparently close to reality.) But he has had little discernible influence on policy.

Peter Mandelson's significance in all this is more difficult to estimate. As Director of Communications under Neil Kinnock, he was undoubtedly important in that period and had a major, though by most accounts not overwhelming hand in the (losing) election campaigns of 1987 and 1992. As Tony Blair's confidant over the post-Kinnock period, he has certainly been significant in the wooing and partial co-opting of the British media on the faction's behalf, especially after Blair took over from John Smith.

On the other hand, how difficult was it to sell 'New Labour'? After 1992, and especially after Smith's death and the arrival of Blair as leader of the party in 1994, the story sold itself. The Tories were going to lose the next election; the next Prime Minister would be Blair; and the 'New Labour' group were ditching the old Labour Party and its policies. That 'New Labour' was anti-union, pro-business, pro-NATO and pro-low corporate and personal taxes, was a message the media's managers and owners were keen to hear and pass on to their audience. No doubt Mandelson had become skilled at doleing out stories to journalists and getting oceans of favourable coverage; but the Conservatives were in disarray and the political journalists had an unlimited appetite for gossip emanating from the Labour leader's office.

All that remained was appeasing Rupert Murdoch. After the 1992 election it was widely believed that Labour had lost the election because of *The Sun's* unremittingly hostile coverage of Labour and of Kinnock in particular. Tony Blair flew to Australia to pledge his allegiance at a meeting of News International's executives in 1995 – what Peter Oborne, now of *The Spectator*, called 'an extraordinary act of fealty'.

Even though they were certain to win the coming election, Gordon Brown promised not to put up income taxes or increase public spending. The City and the financial pages applauded.

And along with all this the Party did go: the scent of victory dulled the senses.

Tony Blair hates the Labour Party. Why did he join it? Because he knew he would rise faster in Labour than in the Tories. He has no interest in democracy or the Labour Party. Both are an impediment. From his earliest days in the Party he wanted to make it resemble the Democrats in America: corporate funding and no irritating members to deal with; no constituency general committees telling MPs how to do things.

A little group ran a con on the Party; and took it over. Since Blair and Brown were the coming men, the next prime minister and chancellor, the Parliamentary Labour Party fell into line. Unity was all. Dissent was anti-party; defeatist. And fatal to career prospects. And since the PLP collectively knows nothing about economics, they had no answer to the neo-conservative lines being run by Brown.

So we let them do it. Many members – most perhaps – refused to believe that they meant what they said. The Party was in collective denial: just as it was in the 80s over the Militant Tendency's penetration of the Party.

The models in the heads of our leaders are all top down: big executives, big offices; management speak. UK PLC; ceo Tony Blair; finance director Gordon Brown. These people are – that old fashioned word – technocrats.

Not terribly bright politicians, fixated on business people while understanding nothing about them or their world. Shortly after their election victory, Blair *et al* met a big delegation of executives. One of the executives came out of the meeting and said, 'We won't have trouble with them: they're star-fuckers.'

But since the model in Blair and Brown's head wasn't the model of most of the Party members, they put out lots of smoke and fudge and even got poor, dear, dim John Prescott to put his seal of approval on it.

And still most members that I know refused to acknowledge what was in their face. There are psychological factors at work here among Party members and people who have resigned from it – denial then, guilt now – which might be worth considering.

I was asked to address 'specific aspects of New Labour which have allowed a tightly knit group of apparatchiks to achieve total power'. Truthfully I'm not sure there are any. New Labour did what any faction – any left faction – would like to do. It's just that they had the combination of circumstances and people to do it:

I don't know how you get the Party back. Having seen what a quiet life it is possible to lead, no future leader will want to return to the days when the leader and the PLP and the NEC fought battles. Only the failure of corporate funding will drive the leader back to the Party.

SPIES

CHAPTER EIGHTEEN

Getting it Right: the Security Agencies in Modern Society

A talk given at the International Centre for Security Analysis [ICSA], London, 2000.

Let me confess at the outset that if the title of this talk seems vague, it is because I couldn't think of a topic. But then I couldn't think of a title for the magazine I publish and let my erstwhile partner call it *Lobster*. He's long gone but I'm stuck with the stupid name . . .

The topic was suggested to me by Kevin O'Brien [of ICSA]. It wasn't clear to me if it was simply that I was being played out a very long piece of rope with which to hang myself. At any rate, given such a wide title – and a title to which I cannot possibly actually do justice – and given my complete lack of knowledge about the audience to whom I am delivering this talk, I decided to chuck out a bunch of ideas in the hope of providing something juicy for you to have a go at. Incidentally, I do actually respond briefly to the stated title at the end of the piece.

A preface: in what follows I use the terms security agencies and secret state to stand for the intelligence and security services – it saves time and endless repetition of a mouthful. Or should I say: I use the term security agencies in place of the intelligence, security and surveillance services, MI6, MI5, GCHQ? Or should I say: I use the term security agencies to stand for the intelligence, security, surveillance and disinformation services? Because disinforming the British citizen is certainly a current aim of at last two of those bodies. Or should it be the intelligence, security, surveillance, disinformation and fucking-up-the-lives-of-certain-people-the-state-finds-embarassing-or-irritating services? Because that, too, is an aim of at least one of the 'security agencies'. To that last category I will return.

I am a generalist not a specialist. I could say that my main interest is in the interface between the political and the intelligence worlds; between secret and authoritarian; between open and democratic. But really I'm just interested in the nature of political and historical reality. I've read Professor Freedman's excellent book on the US intelligence estimating process;[1] but I also read books about UFOs. Both are part of political reality as I see it. Indeed both overlap: the CIA is certainly interested in UFOs. A loose alliance of intelligence officers in America has spent the last 20 years running disinformation at the American UFO buffs. If you have watched *The X Files* TV programme you have been watching themes first invented by this crew. Which is an oblique way into this: the security agencies, the intelligence agencies, are a part of political reality; and maybe a big part – certainly a bigger part than orthodox historians and political scientists would have us believe.

I'm here because I have been publishing a little magazine called *Lobster* for 17 years, part of whose content has information about, and critical commentaries on, the activities of the British and American – mostly British – security agencies. To intelligence professionals, no doubt, the little I have managed to learn and publish is laughable, both in content and quantity. Even so, *Lobster* has had its moments: it has been denounced in the House of Commons by Ray Whitney, former head of the Information Research Department, IRD, the state's official, anti-left, psy-war outfit. Oddly enough this was something he omitted to tell the Commons before denouncing me; not that one MP in 50 would have known what IRD was had he referred to it.

That I am aware of, I have had two agents of the British secret state – from MI5, I presume – sicked onto me to pick my brains. This happened in 1987/8 when I was deeply embroiled with Colin Wallace and his story about anti-Labour hanky panky in Northern Ireland. I was on the phone to him every day and was talking to lots of journalists who were trying to understand his story. Wallace and I assumed our phones were tapped – though we never had any evidence of this: none of the noises, interference and fragments of recorded conversation played back that other people were reporting at that time. Being essentially a one-man band even then – my erstwhile partner Stephen Dorril had abandoned *Lobster* to write a book – *Lobster* must have presented a peculiar problem to an organisation like MI5. How do you penetrate a one-man band? After you have the phone-taps on and the mail intercept, what else is there to do? In the case of something like CND it's easy: someone is sent to join and then volunteer to work at head office. Incidentally, the talk of MI5 'penetrating' CND is a joke: any member could work in head office. It was an open organisation, it ran on volunteers and it had no secrets.

So here we were in 1987: MI5 contemplating what to do about *Lobster*.

What they did was really quite subtle. I was a fairly serious runner then and used to regularly run round the grass perimeter of the University of Hull playing fields. There were three of us running round this field at lunchtimes and eventually we got to talking in the changing rooms, and then went for a beer afterwards; and I became friends with one of them, a post-doc physics researcher, a man called . . . let's call him John. Nice guy: on a similar wavelength to me politically; interesting life; good stories; good drinking companion – and, of course, he was really interested in the little magazine I was publishing and what I was working on. At that point nobody in Hull was interested in what I was doing, not even my girl friend. And I was happy to talk to him. I had no secrets.

About 6 months after I met him, I got a call from an American journalist I know called Jim Hougan. Hougan had been chatting to a friend, who had a contact in the FBI and somehow this little magazine produced in Hull, England, had come up. Don't worry about *Lobster*, was the message: *Lobster* has been penetrated. That seemed absolutely hilarious to Hougan and me. Typical spook bullshit, we thought, claiming to have penetrated an organisation consisting of one man. We had a good laugh

239

down the transatlantic phone line and I forgot about it.

About a month later, as I was cycling through Hull city centre, out of a clear blue sky, without any conscious musings on my part, a voice said to me: 'It must be John' – and about six months experience suddenly reorganised itself in my head. Yes: it was my new running, drinking, talking buddy John. He'd been pretty clever about it, but I knew it was him. I never saw him again.

That, you might think, would be the end of it. Not so. A few weeks went by and another person tried to attach himself to me, this time claiming to be a former MI5 agent who would spill the beans. But he was ill; so ill and the NHS in London was so bad ... This goes on for some weeks and I initially take him seriously and begin badgering doctors in London . . . Then one day he says, 'What's the NHS like in Hull?' Maybe he could move to Hull and get treatment. . . then he would tell me wonderful tales of MI5. At 'moving to Hull' I put the phone down on him. He called himself Sammy. He had been an actor and claimed that MI5 and Special Branch used him to penetrate Left organisations.

Somewhere in Whitehall there must still be files on that operation – a brilliant example of the way our secret state wastes money. Because there was nothing to find out. I had no secret sources: with my mail opened and my phone tapped they knew as much as there was to know.

I have been accused of running Soviet disinformation by Herb Rommerstein, a big cheese in the United States Information Service during the Reagan years. In fact in all the years I have been doing this I have never *seen* a piece of Soviet disinformation. I have seen lots of British and some American disinformation; but even the few examples of Soviet disinformation described by Oleg Gordievsky never came my way. And no-one on the Rommerstein side of things has produced a critique showing me how I had – wittingly or unwittingly – been running Soviet themes through *Lobster*. Perhaps I have; I would be interested to be shown how and where. More recently, I have been accused a couple of times of being a front for MI6 by American conspiracy theory nutters. But that's about par for the course in these fields.

The examples of Soviet disinformation offered by Gordievsky from the 1980s in his book *KGB* were laughably incompetent forgeries which would fool no-one and which had zero distribution as far as I know on this country's Left. And their incompetence brings me to the first point I want to make today.

In the last decade of the the Cold War the Soviet Union – the Soviet state – was portrayed in the West as a vast, chaotic shambles in which nothing worked, all was cheap, second-rate; a state which never managed to produce a decent refrigerator, and whose chosen motor car was the Lada, built on the cast-off assembly line from the Fiat factories. Oddly enough though, in the midst of this ocean of mediocrity there were apparently exceptions – oases of excellence. Somehow the Soviet military and the Soviet intelligence services had escaped the bureaucratic nightmare which was the Soviet command economy and had become the exception which proved

241

the rule: they were efficient and a deadly threat to us. This never seemed likely to me and I was delighted to read the book by the pseudonymous Soviet defector, Viktor Suvorov, called *The Liberators: inside the Soviet Army*. In *The Liberators*, published in London in 1981, Suvorov portrayed the Soviet armed forces I expected to find: a brutal, inefficient, cynical, farcical army of conscripts, skiving off at the first opportunity and doing their best to stay permanently smashed on *anything* they could smoke, drink or inject – the mirror image of wider Soviet society, in short; and about as threatening to NATO as the girl guides.

Alas for Suvorov, his handlers in the British (?) state did not seem happy with this portrayal of the Soviet armed forces and the next year he published – or put his name to – another book whose main title was the subtitle of his previous book: *Inside the Soviet Army*. In the year since *The Liberators*, Mr Suvorov had experienced a dramatic change of memory and his second book presented the efficient, menacing, Red Army required by Western intelligence and military budgets. Suvorov subsequently wrote – or put his name to – a whole slew of books amplifying the Soviet menace in the 1980s. The range of his expertise was astonishing for a relatively junior officer. Flipping through some of those recently, I was reminded of Derek Draper's immortal response to the question, 'Did you actually write your book *New Labour's First 100 Days*?' 'Write it?' said Draper. 'I didn't even read it.'

File the Suvorov episode away as a dramatic example of the way host countries manipulate defectors; and remember his name the next time you read about the new 'threats' facing NATO.

Looking at the West from the position of the free market Right, the state – the public sector – is by definition the quintessence of inefficiency. States are neither rational nor efficient distributors of resources. But where are the free market critics of the security agencies? Where were the shouts of derision from stage right when MI5 and MI6 – so I read – overspent the budgets on their new buildings by £200 million?

What was that £200 million overspend? What did it mean? First, it was hardly an overspend. I might overspend on my weekly budget; you don't overspend by *£200 million*. It's the wrong term: but I'm not sure what the correct term would be in bureaucratic language. The £200 million was a big 'fuck you' to the rest of Whitehall – and the politicians. Whitehall couldn't stop them and didn't bother telling the politicians until it had happened. There was the tiniest squeak of outrage from the House of Commons and the whole thing has been buried. Now MI6 sit on the Thames, in all their architectural, post-modern pomp. Think of the contrast between the days of Menzies – even Oldfield – between the willing embrace of anonymity in the service of the state and nation so beautifully and apparently accurately described by John Le Carré, and today's flashy display. If Menzies and Oldfield thought they were playing the master game at some level, they had the good taste not to flaunt it the way today's MI6 are doing. *That building is taking the piss*; that building is asking to have a grenade fired at it. And the politicians are too afraid to say so.

I mentioned that the so-called overspend of £200 million by our secret servants produced a squeak of outrage from the House of Commons. That squeak came from the the Public Accounts Committee. The committee nominally dealing with our secret servants, the Intelligence and Security Committee, said nothing; and said nothing because it is not *allowed* to say anything not vetted by the FCO – sorry Foreign and Commonwealth Office – and the Home Office. The ISC is *invited* to do x or y.

For example, on the opening page of the ISC report on the Mitrokhin Inquiry, there is the formal letter from ISC chair Tom King which begins:

'Dear Prime Minister, on 13th September 1999 you and the Home Secretary *invited* the Intelligence and Security committee to examine the policies and procedures . . .'

On page 10 we read 'The Home Secretary wrote to the ISC Chairman on 8th October establishing the inquiry's terms of reference . . . '

This what you are allowed to do . . .

While the ISC were being invited to look at Mitrokhin and the way he was handled by MI6, messrs Shayler and Tomlinson, the two most important defectors from the British security agencies since Philby, were in exile in one case, and in jail in the other. While Shayler was sitting in a French jail, the House of Commons had its first debate on the work of the ISC which had produced its first report that summer: neither report nor debate mentioned Shayler.

To my knowledge, no Labour politicians have met either of them; not one. None of the ISC members of course; they are forbidden to talk to either Tomlinson or Shayler unless invited to do so by higher authorities. Yes, while Tomlinson and Shayler talked of assassination plots by employees of HMG, our politicians were sitting in the sand pit, given 50 year-old allegations about Melita Norwood to play with – allegations which, even if true, mattered little in 1950 and mean nothing today.

This is taking the piss.

Which brings me to another of the recurring questions of the past 15 years: why are our politicians so passive in this field? Why do MPs sit on the ISC doing degrading, keep-em-busy, shit-work? Why do MPs take no notice of a £200 million overspend? From a *Conservative* government we would expect nothing else, of course. The security agencies simply are not on their agenda. The Tories are historically the Queen and country party, after all; they have had institutional links with the security agencies for the past 100 years. And while the Tories accept that in general terms the state is often the problem and should be reduced if possible, they also believe that the security agencies are a miraculous exception to the general incompetence of public organisations; are, indeed, paragons of efficiency and virtue which need no supervision. They are splendid chaps, doing a wonderful job. I can hear ISC chair, former Tory Minister of Defence and Secretary of State for Northern Ireland Tom King, saying: 'splendid chaps doing a wonderful job.' Tom King, as they say, isn't the sharpest knife in the kitchen drawer. This may explain why Mr Blair left him in the job when Labour won the election in 1997.

The Labour Party's passivity in the face of the secret state is a more complex phenomenon. Partly it is simply a reflection of wider passivity in the face of the state *per se*. The idea that the British state is a problem has never really been part of the culture of the Labour Party. Despite all the evidence to the contrary, the idea – the myth – of civil service neutrality is believed by the upper echelons of the Labour Party. And there is a distant folk memory of Harold Wilson's attempt to challenge the power of the Treasury in his first government – and his defeat by them. In practice the idea that the state is a problem is too difficult, has too many awkward ramifications, for Labour politicians. And if, say, the power of the civil service in an ordinary government department looks too difficult to challenge, the secret state is simply off the agenda at the Parliamentary Labour Party level.

In the 1980s doing something about the secret state was on the Labour Party' formal agenda – right at the bottom, it is true, but it was on there. It was there because of pressure from ordinary members of the left-wing of the Labour Party – people like me who had read a few books. In those days it was possible for members to actually do things; these days members are just people who fill in standing order forms and work to elect the candidates picked by head office.

There was no real intent by the leadership group around Neil Kinnock, however. To them it was all just noises off stage, rantings from the Left. This changed a little in 1986/87 after the series of revelations from Peter Wright, Colin Wallace and Cathy Massiter which confirmed all but the most paranoid lefty's view of the security agencies' institutional hostility to the Labour Party and Labour movement. For a few moments there, Neil Kinnock even threatened to do something. A member of his personal staff actually phoned *Spycatcher* Peter Wright in Australia in the run-up to the attempt by the British government to stop the publication of Wright's book. It does not seem to have occurred to Kinnock and co. that every phone within a mile of Wright and his legal team was tapped, of course, and the NSA had their resources on the case. The information about the call from Kinnock's office was duly passed – presumably from GCHQ – to the Tories. Mrs Thatcher then stood up in the Commons and denounced Kinnock for talking to a traitor.

It was one of those moments when a little more wit or bottle might have changed things. Kinnock should have laughed at her – but he didn't. He should have asked her how she knew the content of the phone call. But he didn't. He should have derided her talk of treason and pointed out that Wright, a senior member of MI5, was saying that parts of MI5 had been plotting against his party. *He* should have raised the cry of treason. But he didn't. In the event, taunted by Mrs Thatcher, Neil Kinnock panicked, rushed to wrap himself in the flag and declare himself a loyal patriotic Brit; and the whole subject of the security agencies was wiped off the Kinnock team's blackboard; and it has never returned.

Neil Kinnock panicked, and Labour MPs walk away from this field, because they don't know anything. A Neil Kinnock – even an averagely conscientious MP – has so much to do, so much paper to process, that he or she is never going to be able to read enough to master this field. And this field looks uniquely dangerous to MPs, especially on the Left. Nobody with an ounce of career-mindedness is going to take a critical interest in the security agencies. For MPs believe – whether this is a rational belief or not – that the security agencies can destroy them. And in a subject so dangerous, no MP is going to be *advised* what to say. I spent years sending out such advice to Labour MPs: not a word of it was acted on. So: as they don't know what to say or do, they say and do nothing.

It is unclear to me how rational is the belief of MPs that the security agencies could destroy them.[2] It is clear from Colin Wallace's documents that before 1974, MI5 was trawling through MPs' private lives gathering dirt. But evidence of security agency-gathered material wrecking MPs careers is thin. There are some cases in the Wilson period of MPs who wanted to become ministers having their careers blocked by bad refs from MI5. But the MP who has done the most attacking of the security agencies, Ken Livingstone, survived and is now Mayor of London.

On the other hand there is the case of Tom Spencer MEP, who until last year was the leader of the Tory group of MEPs in the European Parliament. I remember getting a call from an MEP's researcher in Brussels asking me who Spencer was. 'Never heard of him,' I replied. 'Why?' It turned out Spencer had been asking questions about a rather sensitive American project whose initials are HAARP, which allegedly links to various mind control and weather modification projects. This was about the only time I made a correct prediction. I said to the researcher something to the effect that Spencer better watch out, because the Yanks would go for him if he continued poking around in that field. And lo and behold, about six months later, Customs just happened to pick his bags to search and just happened to find some cocaine and some porno mags in them. Cue media interest; cue end of Tom Spencer's political career. There is one MP in the Commons who is having a go at the secret state, a Lib-Dem called Norman Baker. If you see smear stories about him you will know whence the stories came.[3]

However, the Wilson plots story of the 1986-9 period, the biggest source of information on the activities of the security agencies in this country in the post-war era came and went; and, despite file drawers full of cuttings, it had virtually no effect on the political system. Nobody was fired; no meaningful structural changes were made to the security agencies. It is said that they were persuaded to broaden the base of their recruitment and rely less on the old boy public school network; but no meaningful political oversight, let alone political control, was introduced.

You can tell that nothing has changed because MI5 and MI6 can spend £200 million more than they should have and get away with it. Indeed they must be thinking: why didn't we spend more? They said nothing about £200 million, maybe we could have had £400 million! The security agencies must love having this lot in office. Utterly ignorant of their activities – and determined to remain ignorant.

For the leadership of the Labour Party, the process of becoming respectable, becoming electable, not only meant not challenging the power of the City of London, it also means not challenging – not even talking about – the secret state.

Of course the subject was never on the agenda of the Blair faction. Within his inner group, we have Peter Mandelson who has been around MI6 since his early 20s, and Jonathan Powell, ex FCO in Washington and, it has been alleged, the MI6 man there, before joining Blair. (For this latter charge there is no evidence, to my knowledge; and I suspect that if it were true, Mr Tomlinson would have found a way to let us know by now.) Four of the Blair Cabinet are alumni of the Anglo-American elite group the British American Project; three of the Blair cabinet have passed muster at Bilderberg meetings; and the entire defence team in Blair's first Cabinet in 1997 were members or associates of the Trade Union Committee for European and Transatlantic Unity, created by the Americans in the 1970s – probably, though not yet provably, created by the CIA – and currently funded by NATO.

Blair, like his Conservative Party counterparts, believes – or pretends to believe – that the security agencies are splendid chaps doing a splendid job who need no supervision from mere politicians . . .

As the publisher of a little magazine interested in this field, I have met a number of whistle-blowers and victims of HMG's secret organisations; and in all the cases of which I have knowledge the same pattern emerges: honest, decent, loyal, patriotic members of this society get screwed because they know something the secret state would rather the rest of us didn't know. The secret state's response to Fred Holroyd, Colin Wallace, John Burnes, Harold Smith, and most recently Shayler and Tomlinson, is always the same.[4] Never mind the content of what they are saying; never mind their previous service to the state, fuck-up their lives. Fred Holroyd was put in a mental hospital. Colin Wallace was framed for manslaughter. Less well known, John Burnes was persecuted by MI5. Persons unknown tried to get him killed by the INLA, then tried to frame him for robbery. A post-grad student at the time, he had his grant withdrawn; and, after training as a teacher, he was blocked by MI5 from teaching. His offence? He had the temerity to fall in love with and marry the wife of Sir Thomas Legg, at the time the Lord Chancellor's Department's liaison with MI5. It was Legg who appointed the judge who oversaw the framing of Colin Wallace. The crazy conspiracy theorists in MI5 concluded that Burnes was a KGB agent who had targetted Legg. At one point Burnes sought political asylum in Holland.

And there is Shayler and Tomlinson . . .

The really stupid thing is that none of these people wanted to blow the whistle, wanted to make trouble. All have been pushed into the role by the incompetent personnel management of our secret servants.

It amazes me that anyone would work for them, so awful are they to work for. Take Jonathan Moyle, a not very bright, gung-ho Queen and country man. Young Moyle, while at University at Aberystwyth, was a Special Branch snitch who thought it his patriotic duty to tell the local SB who was smoking dope. On graduating he became an agent for – well, MI6 probably, though who knows? Moyle ended up being murdered in Chile. According to the book about him, Moyle wasn't very subtle as an intelligence asset and was poking around the Chilean arms dealer Cardoen – allegedly a business associate of Mark Thatcher's friends – while Cardoen was doing a big helicopter deal with the Iraqis. This was in the run-up to the American attack on Iraq. Moyle ended up dead in a wardrobe in Chile and what does the local FCO guy do? Tells the media that Moyle was the victim of an auto-erotic accident: strangled himself while having a wank.

There is lot of this about, apparently. James Rusbridger, the writer on intelligence, apparently died this way; and so, apparently, did Tory MP Stephen Milligan, PPS to

Jonathan Aitken. Does my nose wrinkle at this? Just a bit, I have to confess.

Maybe there are people here thinking of working for the secret departments of HMG. My advice would be consider the experience of Moyle, John Burnes and Colin Wallace before you do.

One of the major themes of Colin Wallace was the internecine conflicts in Northern Ireland between MI5, MI6, the RUC Special Branch and the Army. These conflicts are still going on. There was a major outbreak of leaks – i.e. of official secrets – to the press in the early 1990s when the Special Branch was trying to resist MI5's take-over of the anti-terrorism franchise. MI5 won. Part of the reason for MI5's hatred of David Shayler is his revelation of just how incompetent MI5 were in dealing with the IRA in the UK, having won that franchise.

Currently there is a major struggle going on between the RUC Special Branch and the Army, with the RUC leaking to the *Sunday Times* the details of the campaign of assassinations in Northern Ireland by the Army's Force Research Unit, the FRU. A barrow-load of official secrets have been exposed in this one. We have the extraordinary situation in which one arm of the British secret state is trying to bust the journalist concerned, Liam Clarke, for leaking information given to him by another of the state's secret arms.

Meanwhile, MI6 have returned to planting disinformation in the British media – most of it that I can see is going into the *Sunday Telegraph*. Tomlinson told us about the 20-strong I/Ops – Information Operations – unit in that shiny building on the Thames. But its existence had been visible for a long time. It is increasingly difficult to take the talk of official secrets seriously. *The Sunday Telegraph* of 24 September carried two pieces from MI6. There was a puff piece by former MI6 officer Alan Petty, using his *nom de plume* Alan Judd, on the MI6 building in the wake of the IRA attack on it; and there was the latest in the long line of anti-Gaddafi pieces claiming that Libya now has some North Korean ballistic missiles. The only stated source for the allegation was a 'Western intelligence official'. But four months before, on 28 May 2000, *The Sunday Times* article 'IRA investors make 300% profit out of Gaddafi cash donations', sourced back to 'MI5 documents seen by *The Sunday Times*', concluded by telling us that Swiss police were 'investigating the supply to Libya from *Taiwan* of plans and parts for Scud missiles.' Well, does Gaddafi have Taiwanese Scuds (MI5 story planted in *The Sunday Times*) or North Korean missiles (MI6 story planted in *The Sunday Telegraph*)?

Sometimes these MI6 planted stories are really laughable. *The Sunday Telegraph* of 30 July carried a story by Christina Lamb, 'Diplomatic Correspondent' which claimed that Saddam Hussein had sent belly-dancing assassins to London to murder his opponents there. Lamb sourced this to 'a Foreign Office official' – the traditional euphemism for MI6.

This may seem comic, frivolous, even – at worst a waste of public money. But it's more serious than that. *The Sunday Times* was a serious, respectable newspaper until the mid-1980s when it turned into the mouthpiece for MI5 and the MOD to run their rubbish through. *The Sunday Telegraph* shows all the signs of going down the same dangerous path. But then I'm an old-fashioned kind of a person who thinks the quality and independence of our mass media is important.

If patriotism is the last refuge of the scoundrel, to quote Dr Johnson, secrecy is the first refuge of the incompetent – or the illegal. Because this is the issue. The suspicion of people like me is that the security agencies want secrecy to cover their incompetence and their featherbedding; and also to conceal activities they would rather we didn't know – activities they shouldn't be engaged in. MI6 is not supposed to be in the business of assassinating foreign leaders, even if that leader is on the Americans shit list like Milosevic. MI5 is not supposed to be in the business of collecting and distributing the dirt on British MPs – which is what they were doing in the 1970s. What else have they been doing, free from the gaze of politicians and journalists? At root, I suspect what they are most keen to conceal is the extent to which they have been working in, manipulating, civil society. The Wilson plots story was an example of these activities erupting into the public gaze.

At each step as the police increase their powers, we hear 'If you are innocent you have nothing to fear'. Anybody who has been half-awake in the last 20 years knows that this is simply nonsense; that many – dozens, maybe hundreds – of the innocent have been routinely framed and incarcerated by our legal system. But this statement can be levelled at the security agencies: if what you have been doing is above board, show us the files. Take out the agents' name – fine. Nobody expects to see them. But for the rest . . . Of course it won't happen, not here; not with politicians as docile and cowed as the ones we currently have.

It is absolutely typical of this society that the recent legislation passed which – allegedly – will protect whistle-blowers, does not encompass the heart of the state: police, military, intelligence. It is absolutely typical that the security agencies have been given blanket immunity from the provision of the Data Protection Act. It is also absolutely typical of our security agencies that rather than be less secretive, less authoritarian, less vindictive, less illegal and less bloody incompetent, they are going to introduce psychometric testing of their employees to try and weed out any future Shaylers and Tomlinsons.

Finally, to return to the title of this talk, 'The security agencies: Getting it right in modern society', in one sense MI6 and MI5 have got it right, are in fact, a brilliant success. Faced with their biggest crisis of the post-war period, the end of the Red Menace which justified the budgets, the careers and the gongs, they have emerged with budgets renewed, new agendas approved; untouched by the politicians, unsupervised by anyone, still – we are not supposed to laugh – still accountable to the Crown not Parliament (i.e. to no-one). Both MI6 and MI5 have reacted to the new conditions post Cold War in thoroughly competent, even creative ways. Needing something to justify the budget, MI6 picked the international drug trade. Far as I know, since MI6 joined the 'war against drugs', the price of cocaine and heroin in the UK at street level has halved: it is now cheaper to get off your face, as they say in Hull, on smack than it is on alcohol. And didn't I read a few months ago that MI6 had persuaded Clare Short – she of the big mouth, big heart and little brain – to task them to provide her with early warning of coups in the developing world? An honest-to-goodness license to do anything, anywhere. Only a Labour government, timid and ignorant, would fall for a proposal as preposterous as that one.

MI5 hardly paused for breath after losing the KGB 'threat' contained in the Soviet Embassy and its Trade Mission, before acquiring the domestic terrorism franchise from the Met Special Branch and beginning the process of hyping-up the animal rights and green activists as a new terrorist threat. (And they are getting a new definition of terrorism run through the Houses of Parliament to support it.)

Of course, only the politicians and some of the media – the handful who are paying any attention at all – take the talk of the war on drugs seriously. MI6 don't, I am sure; any more than they seriously intend to provide Clare Short with an early warning of coups in the Third World. At the higher levels of MI6, MI5 and all the rest they must be chortling in the senior dining rooms at the incredible gullibility of the British political class – and this present lot in particular.

Notes

1 Lawrence Freedman, *U.S. Intelligence and the Soviet strategic threat* (London: Macmillan, 1986). Professor Freedman was head of King's College, to which the ICSA is attached.

2 One example was Lord (Nicholas) Bethell whose career as a minister in the Conservative government of Edward Heath was ended by suspicions in MI5 that he might be a security risk. Not, please note, that he had been a security risk; merely that he might become one. See his obituary in *The Times* at http://www.timesonline.co.uk/to1/comment/obituaries/article24226135.ece

3 Thus far, there has not been any sign of a smear campaign against Norman Baker MP, though he has reported that one of his computers was 'remotely wiped'. See http://news.bbc.co.uk/1/hi/england/southern_counties/517830.stm

4 Harold Smith was a British civil servant in Nigeria who witnessed and objected to the British authorities rigging the first post-independence election in that country, which led to the war in Biafra and millions of deaths. Attempting to blow the whistle on this, he wrecked his career. I published an account of this in *Lobster* 25 (1993). More accessible, just Google 'Harold Smith + Nigeria'.

CHAPTER NINETEEN

Researching the Secret State

This talk was given to a summer school for investigative journalism, Westminster University, July 2003.

I was told to talk about researching the British secret state. Apparently I have done this. But I wouldn't claim to have ever 'researched the British secret state'. I have read a lot of books and articles on the subject. I have researched some of what's been *published* about the secret, or maybe that should be not-quite-so-secret, state.

Some of this explosion of information occurred after the fall of the Soviet empire. Bereft of their traditional opponents, the spooks were forced to raise their public profile in bids to find new roles to justify their budgets. But some of the information appeared before 1989, during the years of Margaret Thatcher, who hated people like us; who would probably think it a kind of treason even to attend this talk; and who thought almost everything should be secret.

Here is a measure of how things have changed.

Gordon Brook-Shepherd is a journalist who used to write about foreign affairs and intelligence, chiefly for the *Telegraph*. He is the author of a pair of books about intelligence history which were obviously written with the assistance of MI6, *The Storm Birds* and *The Storm Petrels*. The author blurb on his *The Storm Petrels*, published in 1988, described him as having 'a deep understanding of the world of espionage' (hint, hint) and as being a 'much-travelled foreign correspondent' (hint, hint).

In his latest book, *The Iron Maze: the Western Secret Services and the Bolsheviks*, published a decade later in 1998, he remarks on page 2 of his 'two volumes on Soviet defectors to the West (a project *also launched on my behalf by British intelligence*)'; and the blurb on the book jacket says that after a wartime career in military intelligence, Brook-Shepherd became a journalist. 'His first civil post-war post, as head of the *Daily Telegraph's* Central and South-East European Bureau during the Cold War Years, brought him again in touch with the Western intelligence community. These contacts were renewed at intervals right down to the war in Afghanistan, which he covered on the spot when Deputy Editor of the *Sunday Telegraph.*'

In ten years we have gone from nudge, nudge to bragging about links with the spooks.

At first sight, Thatcher presiding over this explosion of knowledge looks like irony. But the increasing information about the secret state and the dominance of neo-liberal economics and reactionary domestic policies are linked. Thatcher used the secret state to help her defeat the Left and the trade unions. She turned the spooks loose, really; they knew they had her support in general terms; she wasn't going to encourage critical scrutiny of her secret servants; nor look too closely at their budgets. But as well as sexy new buildings – hundreds of millions of pounds over budget, of course – and a more prominent role in Whitehall, this expansion of influence by the secret state produced tensions – turbulence is the word they use themselves. Not everybody supported Thatcher's aims, or thought the agencies should be doing some of the things they were doing. So we got whistle-blowers, leaks from within the system: notably Colin Wallace and Fred Holroyd telling us about the secret state's activities in Northern Ireland; Cathy Massiter and Peter Wright from MI5; and, after Thatcher had gone, Richard Tomlinson from 6 and David Shayler from MI5.

These whistleblowers have one thing in common, inci-dentally: none of them have been asked to talk to the House of Commons Intelligence and Security Comm-ittee. The last people our parliamentarians would be allowed to talk to are critics from within the system.

Another source of information since 1980 has been disputes between agencies. Northern Ireland has been a source of some of this: MI5 v MI6 in the 1970s, which we learned of in the mid 1980s; MI5 v Special Branch v the Army more recently.

After the collapse of the Soviet empire, and the collapse of the British Left and trade union movement as serious opponents of capital, the intelligence and secu-rity 'game' changed. MI5 and MI6 had to go looking for new work. MI5 began the post-Red menace era by trying to generate domestic 'threats' to justify its continued existence; but the green movement and the anti-roads and the animal welfare groups hardly constituted an equivalent to the intelligence services of the Soviet bloc. Throughout 1994 the Metropolitan Police and MI5 waged a press war as MI5 tried to move in on turf hitherto occupied by the police. For the first time in this country the politics of intelligence and security agency budgeting were being acted out – in part – in public. Even *The Daily Telegraph* was moved to comment on 5 November 1994 on 'a burst of activity among defence institutions scurrying to identify new roles for themselves to justify their budgets and bureaucracies.'

MI6 acquired 'the war on drugs' franchise as well as international organised crime, though what any of this amounted to we don't know. London appears to be full of gangsters and the price of smack is at an all-time low, as far as I know. So MI6 haven't done much, if anything.

Recently we have had the dispute between Customs and Excise and the rest of the state over the Customs' right to investigative independence.

Most importantly, we are in the midst of a torrent of leaks about the intelligence process before the Iraq war. The Americans are making the British state and politicians pay a heavy price for the privilege of being America's ally. This would be the greatest crisis for the British secret state in my lifetime – if the politicians knew enough about these subjects to ask the right questions and had the bottle to do so.[1] Alas, they don't. But then our politicians are reluctant to go near the secret state: it's bad for their careers.

And the result of all this is that there is now a great deal of information; and if you have the patience, like my former colleague Stephen Dorril, you can pull it together into an enormous book on MI6. Dorril's book exemplifies the current paradox: a thousand pages, with hundreds of footnotes to thousands of other pages, on the supposedly secret intelligence service.

So, yes, you can sort of research the British secret state by reading the books and the newspapers; and if you read enough you will acquire a feel for the subject and maybe have a sense of what is going on; or was going on when the books were written. But if you were told by an editor to research – say – MI6's current psy-ops operations in the British media, what would you do? Where would you go? Maybe you have a connection to a spook; you think he or she is going to talk about this? Give you leads? If you found the name of one of the MI6 officers in the unit, he or she wouldn't talk to you and your inquiry would almost certainly result in persons unknown and unidentified taking an interest in you; and possibly taking steps to screw-up your life. There are civil servants, paid for by us, whose job it is to screw up peoples' lives – people designated as enemies of the state, in effect. Publishing the kind of magazine I do, some of the victims of this stuff come to me when the major media declines to take an interest.

In real terms, in pursuit of MI6's current media operations, you would probably get no further than columns of *The Sunday Telegraph* which prints lots of the MI6 output; and even then, obvious though some of the MI6 plants in the *Telegraph* are, it would be very difficult to prove they were that.

These days, it is *The Sunday Telegraph* which is most obviously running spook stories. In the 1980s the major transmitter of secret state disinformation, mostly from MI5, was *The Sunday Times*, among whose many disgraceful smear campaigns those against Arthur Scargill and the unfortunate Carmen Proetta, who witnessed the SAS execution of the three IRA members on Gibraltar, remain in the memory. I don't read *The Sunday Times* carefully enough these days to say how much disinformation is being run through it.

Obvious though this stuff is when you start to look for it, it was useful to get confirmation of this aspect of the spooks' relationship with the media from the former MI6 officer Richard Tomlinson, who told us that 'MI6 devotes considerable resources to lobbying its position in Whitehall, and has a specialised department whose role is to spin-doctor the media by wining and dining favoured journalists and editors.'[2]

Tomlinson let it be known that Dominic Lawson, the then editor of *The Spectator*, was a paid asset of MI6. Lawson and MI6 denied this; but they would, wouldn't they? If true, it would be an interesting example of the changing world (alternatively, of declining standards.) For before the fall of the Soviet Union, the editor of a conservative – big and small C – magazine like *The Spectator* could have been relied upon to open its columns to (dis)information from MI6 out of a sense of patriotism and duty; and wouldn't require a fee. But with the Cold War over, most of the City of London now foreign-owned, Britain now merely a region of the European

Union on the one hand and America's little gofer on the other, the old discourse of nation and state within which concepts like 'duty' and 'national interest' were meaningful, is in disarray. What is 'the national interest' these days? Who is the enemy?

Which isn't to say that you cannot acquire sources within – or close to – the intelligence and security services. But the relationships which ensue will be weighted in favour of the intelligence officer. If they are talking to you it will be on their terms.

And the secret state isn't just the spooks. The police, the military and the judiciary are largely secret. The material you can see in *The Sunday Telegraph* is just the tip of the iceberg of state PR. In 1998, the Ministry of Defence employed 160 PR staff, many of whom will have been through the Army's pys-ops training courses.[3] The line between public relations, spin-doctoring, and running psy-ops campaigns is often so faint as to be invisible.

Like most people my age I'm stuck: my ideas haven't changed much recently. In the early 1980s it seemed to to me that Britain was a profoundly secretive society, in which all the key state functions – law and order, defence, security and intelligence – were carefully excluded from our gaze, let alone our scrutiny. 20 years later a little has changed: but not much. We know a little about the secret state – but have no right to know. We now have an elaborate charade of accountability – but no-one is actually accountable. We have a parliamentary committee – but its agenda is set by the state, not by itself.

In the twenty years I was simultaneously a member of the Labour Party and writing and publishing in this field, only one Labour MP contacted me for information. How many journalists are there in this country working full-time in this area from any kind of critical perspective?

The economist John Kenneth Galbraith was enthusing to US President Lyndon Johnson about an economics lecture he had given: 'John', said Johnson, 'a speech on economics is a bit like pissing down your leg: it feels hot to you at the time but nobody notices'.

The same is true of these fields, most of the time.

Notes

1 In 2006 it was over 200. See Hélène Mulholland, 'Tories attack soaring cost of government PR', *The Guardian*, August 30, 2006

APPENDIX

Uncle Sam's New Labour

First published in Variant issue 6, Autumn 1998, variantmag@btinternet.com

'The New Labour project has always been defined in an Anglo-American context.' [1]

Gordon Brown used to tell interviewers that he spent his summer holidays in the library at Harvard University. In 1986, CND member Tony Blair went on one of those US-sponsored trips to America that are available for promising MPs and came back a supporter of the nuclear deterrent.[2] Blair, Brown and John Monks, an important Blair ally as head of the TUC, have all attended meetings of the Bilderberg group, one of the meeting places of the European-American trans-national elite.[3] David Miliband, Blair's head of policy, did a Masters degree at the Massachusetts Institute of Technology.[4] Jonathan Powell, Blair's foreign policy adviser, is a former Foreign Office official whose previous posting was in the British Embassy in Washington.[5] Ed Balls, Gordon Brown's economics adviser, studied at Harvard, wrote editorials for the *Financial Times*, and was about to join the World Bank before he joined Brown.[6] His wife, 1997 MP Yvette Cooper, also studied at Harvard. Sue Nye, Gordon Brown's personal assistant, lives with Gavyn Davies, chief economist with the American bankers, Goldman Sachs, and one of Labour's chief economic advisers.[7] Marjorie Mowlam, now Secretary of State for Northern Ireland, did a PhD at the University of Iowa and then taught in the United States in the 1970s.[8] Chris Smith, now Heritage Minister, was a Kennedy Scholar in the USA – as were David Miliband and Ed Balls.[9]

And then there's Peter Mandelson, Blair's confidant, chief strategist and, as this was being written, Minister without Portfolio. By the end of his final year at Oxford University in 1976, via the United Nations Association, Mandelson had become Chair of British Youth Council.[10] The British Youth Council began as the British section of the World Assembly of Youth (WAY), which was set up and financed by the CIA and SIS in the early 1950s to combat the Soviet Union's youth fronts.[11] By Mandelson's time in the mid-1970s – under a Labour Government – the British Youth Council was said to be financed by the Foreign Office, though that may have been a euphemism for SIS. Peter Mandelson, we were told in 1995 by Donald McIntyre in the *Independent*, is 'a pillar of the two blue-chip foreign affairs think-tanks, Ditchley Park and Chatham House.'[12]

Peter Mandelson, Majorie Mowlam, Defence Minister George Robertson, Heritage Minister Chris Smith, and junior Foreign Office Minister in the House of Lords, Elizabeth Symons, are all members of the British-American Project for a Successor Generation (BAP), the latest in the long line of American-funded networks which promote American interests among the British political elite.[13] The

BAP newsletter for June/July 1997 headlined its account of the May 1997 General Election, 'Big Swing to BAP'.

An older and more direct expression of American influence within the wider British labour movement is the Trade Union Committee for European and Transatlantic Understanding (TUCETU). TUCETU is the successor to the Labour Committee for Transatlantic Understanding (LCTU), which was set up in 1976 by the late Joe Godson, Labour Attaché at the US embassy in London in the 1950s who had become an intimate of the then leader of the party, Hugh Gaitskell. Organised by two officials of the NATO-sponsored Atlantic Council, TUCETU incorporates Peace Through NATO, the group central to Michael Heseltine's MoD campaign against CND in the early 1980s, and receives over £100,000 a year from the Foreign Office. TUCETU chair Alan Lee Williams was a Labour defence minister in the Callaghan Government, before he defected to the SDP; director Peter Robinson runs the National Union of Teachers' education centre at Stoke Rochford near Grantham. In the mid-1980s Williams and Robinson were members of the European policy group of the Washington Centre for Strategic and International Studies. Among the senior union and Labour Party figures on the TUCETU's 1995 notepaper were Doug McAvoy, general secretary of the National Union of Teachers; CPSA general secretary Barry Reamsbottom (a member of the Successor Generation Project discussed above) and president Marion Chambers; Lord Richard, Labour leader in the House of Lords; former trade union leaders Bill Jordan (now head of the International Confederation of Free Trade Unions, the

CIA's chief Cold War labour movement operation),[14] Lord (Eric) Hammond, and Lord (Frank) Chapple.[15]

The Atlantic Council/TUCETU network provided New Labour's Ministry of Defence team. Defence Secretary George Robertson was a member of the Council of the Atlantic Committee from 1979-90; Lord Gilbert, Minister of State for Defence Procurement, is listed as TUCETU vice chair; Dr John Reid, Minister of State for the Armed Forces, spoke at a TUCETU conference; and MoD press office biographical notes on junior Defence Minister John Speller state that he 'has been a long standing member of the Trade Union Committee for European and Transatlantic Understanding'. Peter Mandelson has written a (very dull) pamphlet for TUCETU based on a speech he gave to its 1996 conference.

In other words, the people round Blair, the key New Labour 'project' personnel, are all linked to the United States, or the British foreign policy establishment, whose chief aim, since the end of the Second World War, has been to preserve the Anglo-American 'special relationship' to compensate for long-term economic decline.

'We asked the Americans . . .'

Mr Blair has been quite open about the US role in all this. To the annual conference of Rupert Murdoch's News Corp he said:

> '. . . the Americans have made it clear they want a special relationship with Europe, not with Britain alone. If we are to be listened to seriously in Washington or Tokyo, or the Pacific, we will often be acting with the rest of Europe . . . the Labour

*Government I hope to lead will be outward-looking, interna-
tionalist and committed to free and open trade, not an outdated
and misguided narrow nationalism.'*[16]

It could hardly be more specific: we asked the Americans
and they said go with Europe and free trade. In other words,
go with traditional, post-war American foreign policy objectives; and, since the mid-1960s, the objectives of the British
overseas lobby. Put another way: thanks to the massive
exportation of British capital which began during the
Thatcher years, British-based capital has the largest overseas
investments after America, and we will continue to support
American political and military hegemony as the best protection for those interests. This is being 'outward-looking' –
looking beyond Britain to where British capital has gone.

But British economic policy being 'outward-looking,
internationalist and committed to free and open trade', in
Blair's words, is precisely the problem from which non-
metropolitan Britain has suffered for most of this century.
These are the values of the overseas lobby, the Home
Counties financial elite, people for whom Hull or Norwich,
let alone Glasgow and Cardiff, are far away places about
which they know nothing – and care about as much.

The analysis of the Labour policy review group chaired
by Byan Gould MP – and that of the many other similar
analyses which preceded it – implied that Labour, if it
sought acceptability from British capitalism, should look
to the domestic economy, to a more radical version of the
producers' alliance attempted by the governments of
Wilson, Callaghan and Heath. But John Smith and Majorie

Mowlam did not embark on a tour of the regional offices of the CBI, or the Chambers of Commerce of the British cities. They headed for the Square Mile. The Blairites, following the lead of John Smith, have become the party of the City, the big trans-national corporations and the Foreign Office – the overseas lobby. They have become the party of the Europe Union – British membership of which is still supported by a majority of the overseas lobby in Britain.[17] This shift explains the enthusiasm for the Blair faction expressed by the London establishment – the Foreign Office, the higher media and the EU-oriented section of British capital – in the run-up to the General Election of 1997. Labour under the Blair faction was a more reliable bet for continued EU membership than the Conservative Party with its vociferous Eurosceptic wing.[18] And with this shift to an overseas orientation, comes the concomitant position that Labour's traditional constituency – so-called Old Labour – the domestic economy, especially manufacturing and the public sector, becomes merely a collection of special interest groups to be taken for granted, conned, betrayed or ignored.

The problem becomes the solution

The key move was to see the City – the overseas lobby – and the asset-stripping of the domestic economy, which began in the 1980s, not as the problem but as the solution. This shift can be illustrated by two quotations. The first is from the Labour Party policy document, *Meet the Challenge Make the Change: A new agenda for Britain*, the final report of Labour's Policy Review for the 1990s, published in 1989. The subsection 'Finance for Industry' (p. 13), began:

'Under-investment is the most obvious symptom of short-termism in our economic affairs, yet there is no shortage of funds for investment purposes. The problem lies in the criteria by which the City judges investment opportunities. If short-termism is the disease, then it is the City which is the source of the infection.'

This section is a rewrite by what Austin Mitchell MP called 'the leadership'[19] of a section of the document written by the committee chaired by Bryan Gould. The original Gould committee version had stated, *inter alia*:

'The concentration of power and wealth in the City of London is the major cause of Britain's economic problems'; and that Britain's economic policy had for too long 'been dominated by City values and run in the interests of those who hold assets rather than those who produce.'[20]

Seven years later in their *The Blair Revolution*, Peter Mandelson and co-author Roger Liddle, now Tony Blair's adviser on Europe, said of Britain in the 1990s:

'Britain can boast of some notable economic strengths – for example, the resilience and high internationalisation of our top companies, our strong industries like pharmaceuticals, aerospace, retailing and media; the pre-eminence of the City of London.' [21]

Not only has the City ceased to be the problem it was perceived to be nine years before, Mandelson and Riddle have internalised the values of the overseas sector of the economy, of which the City is the core. Not only is the 'high

273

internationalisation' of our top companies an 'economic strength', we now have a retailing 'industry' and media 'industry'.

Good-bye manufacturing

The prospect of North Sea oil revenues had begun to persuade members of the overseas lobby that they could, perhaps, abandon what they saw as the troublesome, union-ridden, manufacturing sector of the economy. In 1978, we learn from Frank Blackaby, that a 'senior Treasury official' had commented, 'Perhaps we can either have North Sea oil or manufacturing industry, but not both.' [22] On 3 July 1980, Samuel Brittan, who was then the leading economic commentator on the right of British politics, published an article in the *Financial Times* headed, 'Deindustrialisation is good for the UK.' The former Thatcher Minister, the late Nicholas Ridley, wrote in his memoir:

> *'I do not think it is a disaster if we become an economy based primarily on the service sector. It isn't vital, as socialists seem to think, that we have a large manufacturing sector. They seem to think this mainly because Britain's old manufacturing industries used to be the basis of their political support.'* [23]

The former Conservative Minister, Cecil Parkinson, one of Mrs Thatcher's Ministers at the Department of Trade and Industry, wrote in his memoir:

> *'Trade [i.e. Ministry for Trade at the DTI] traditionally took the view that it was the custodian of GATT and*

274

upholder of the open market wherever possible. It tried to ensure that we acted within the rules of GATT and was sometimes regarded as almost unpatriotic when it argued the case that just because other people's imports were unwelcome this was not necessarily unfair.' [24]

Whereas a domestically-oriented Department of Trade might see its role as promoting British exports, defining its role as the 'the upholder of the open market' is as clear an expression of the overseas lobby's views as can be imagined.

As the Thatcher regime accelerated the deindustrialisation of Britain, this was rationalised in and around the City of London and by some of its spokespersons in the Tory Party, notably Chancellor of the Exchequer Nigel Lawson, with the belief that financial and other services would replace manufacturing industry: we were moving to a post-industrial society, such as . . . Switzerland?[25]

During John Major's period as Prime Minister, Edward Pearce wrote:

'I have been told by a Treasury knight that though very fond of Mr Major, he worried a little at his anxiety about manufacturers. "He wasn't very happy with the analogies we made about Switzerland, so prosperous entirely from service industries, so it was necessary to let him make friendly things (sic) to the manufacturing people."' [26]

Pearce is telling us that one of the most senior civil servants at the Treasury, and by implication – the use of 'we' – perhaps several or all of them, had decided that Britain should pursue a policy of abandoning its manufacturing base altogether.[27]

One of Gordon Brown's appointments to the Bank of England Monetary Policy Committee, the American economist DeAnne Julius, was the co-author of an essay which argued that it would be a mistake for Western governments to try and hang on to their manufacturing base and that they should concentrate on service industries.[28] (And according to William Keegan in *The Observer* 15 February 1998, Ms Julius is 'widely considered to be the closest the MPC [Monetary Policy Committee] has to someone in touch with industry.'!)

Such attitudes are now openly expressed in the financial media. Gavyn Davies is perhaps Labour's most important economic advisor. He lives with Gordon Brown's office manager, Sue Nye, and is the chief economist for the US bank Goldman Sachs. Immediately after the Labour election victory in 1997 he dismissed concern about the damage the rising pound was doing to British exporters, with the comment that "that the health of the one sector of the economy which is directly affected by the exchange rate [i.e. domestic manufacturing] cannot take precedence over the maintenance of the inflation target.' [29] (Davies' implied claim that the City is not 'directly affected by the exchange rate' is an extraordinary lie or self-delusion. The higher it is the more money the City makes.) By early 1998 Davies' response had become the standard reply to all complaints about the value of sterling.

The same line was offered in the *Daily Telegraph* in 1998 in an article whose title, 'Metal bashers shut up shop and do the nation a service', echoed that of Samuel Brittan's 'De-industrialisation is good for Britain' nearly twenty years before:

> 'Sympathy for manufacturers is no basis for economic policy...the plain fact is that manufacturing will go on shrinking, and the more prosperous we become, the faster it will decline . . . interest rates may be relatively high, but setting them in order to succour manufacturing will only succeed in feeding inflation.' [30]

With these attitudes comes the extension of the term 'industry' to encompass any kind of economic activity. We now have 'service industries', 'financial industries', 'leisure industries', 'the sports industry', 'the tourism industry', 'the gambling industry', 'the sex industry' etc etc. It does not matter if the manufacture of products in Britain declines: they will continue to be replaced by financial 'products', holiday 'products', leisure 'products' and so forth. (As yet I haven't noticed welfare 'products' but they cannot be far off now.)

New Labour's economic policy makes no distinction between the City and domestic manufacturing. But policies which suit the domestic economy – cheap money, expansion, controls on the uses of money and credit; planning, consistent demand in the economy – do not suit the City which wants expensive money (sorry: 'competitive interest rates') and freedom from controls (sorry: 'self regulation'). This used to be understood by the Labour Party and was the basis of party economic policy until the mid 1980s.[31]

New Labour still occasionally recognises that there is something called the domestic manufacturing economy, and as the value of sterling rose throughout the first year of New Labour's first term in government with the steady dose of increase rate rises imposed by the newly independent Bank of England, government spokespersons initially watched from the wings and made ritual noises of sympathy and regret – what the unnamed Treasury official quoted above called 'making friendly things to the manufacturing people.'

- 'Mr Brown...is concerned that sterling's 20% appreciation over the past 12 months will damage industry by making exports more expensive.' [32]
- Helen Liddell, Economic Secretary to the Treasury: 'We share the concern about the impact the pound has on industry.' [33]
- President of the Board of Trade, Margaret Beckett: 'The Government values the manufacturing base of this country and shares its belief in the benefits of a stable and competitive exchange rate.' [34]

But three months later Mrs Beckett told the annual dinner of the Engineering Employers' Federation that the government 'has to take a view of across the whole economy, not just a part, even as important a part as manufacturing' – the line offered by Gavyn Davies, quoted above.[35]

A fatal inversion?

British politics has been stood on its head. The Conservative Party, traditionally the party of financial and overseas interests, has been replaced in that role by Labour. Instructed by its new friends in the City, Labour has become the party of financial, pre-Keynesian, orthodoxy. Gordon Brown looks determined to reenact the role of Philip Snowden in 1931 – the perfect Labour Party front man for the interests of the overseas lobby. The last three years of the Major regime saw Chancellor Kenneth Clarke running the kind of orthodox demand management policy – increasing government deficits in response to the recession – which Labour, under Wilson or Callaghan, would have run, but which is anathema to 'Iron Chancellor' Brown. On becoming Chancellor, virtually his first action was to make the Bank of England independent; and the Bank of England said, 'Thanks very much' and began putting interest rates up, despite the pound being too high for the domestic manufacturing economy. The first year of New Labour's term of office produced a stream of newspaper stories complaining of the damage being done to British manufacturing by the strength of sterling identical to those which appeared in the first years of Mrs Thatcher's Government – and for the same reason: interest rates were being put up.[36] Once again, just as in the first years of the Thatcher regime, the exchange rate for sterling was not a consideration.

Gordon Brown gave up the state's influence on the Bank of England, as far as we can tell, in the belief that independent central banks have a better record on preventing inflation than those under political control.[37] Which is another way of saying that, without prioritising the effects on the domestic economy, central banks can be relied on to put interest rates up. Gordon Brown acts as though he's got the equivalent of economic amnesia, and cannot remember anything that happened before 1997. How else can we explain his determination to try to 'control' inflation using only interest rates – what Edward Heath used to dismiss as 'one club golf' – and ignoring the large range of other economic tools which were used, in the days before Mrs Thatcher?

We are powerless

'New Labour' believes – but is unwilling to state in so many words – that governments can do nothing against the power of trans-national finance. This belief has become the acid test for 'New Labour'. In the Commons debate on the Nick Leeson-Barings debacle on 27 February 1996, it was Sir Peter Tapsell, a High Tory stockbroker, not Shadow Chancellor Gordon Brown or Labour's City spokesman Alastair Darling, who declared that the derivatives market was 'so speculative in nature as to deserve the term gambling and perhaps should be banned in international law.' Gordon Brown meekly echoed Chancellor of the Exchequer Kenneth Clarke and called for an inquiry. In a letter to me on the subject of Tapsell's remarks on derivatives, Alastair Darling, now Chief Secretary to the Treasury, made the following assertions:

'It is not possible to ban derivatives. They have been about for 200 or 300 years. Properly controlled and supervised there nothing per se wrong with them. The fault lies in the control systems. In any event, I trust that you will accept that it would be impossible for one country to ban the trade even if

it was desirable. The trade would need to be banned throughout the world.'

To the implicit question, 'Why not do something about this?' Darling replied:

It cannot be done. (So do nothing.) *In any case, there is nothing wrong with them.* (So do nothing.) *Even if there was, and you wanted to ban them, it would have to be done world-wide.* (So do nothing.)

The financial sector's interest in not being controlled by government has been universalised into the beliefs that not only is it impossible to impose such control, it is positively a bad thing to try. (The market is magic.) In an article in *The Times*, Peter Riddell said what the politicians never quite dare to say: 'Politicians know that real power lies with global business.' But where is the evidence to support this belief? Where is the evidence to support the view that the nation state can no longer manage its own economy? When you ask you usually get told of the 'French failure' in 1983, when the Mitterand Government tried to expand the economy in a pretty traditional demand management fashion – while trying to remain a member of the European Monetary System. But as an example of the impossibility of demand management in one economy, this example fails. Just as Heath did in 1972 with his expansion, the French government reached the point where they either floated the currency as the trade balance went into deficit, or abandoned the expansion. Pursuit of the geopolitical competition with Germany inside the then EEC, the so-called 'franc fort' policy, proved more important, and the French government abandoned the expansion.[38] Thus, it is believed on all sides, did 'Keynesianism in one country' die. But even the most lumpen accounts of demand management economics acknowledge that it may be necessary to abandon attempts to maintain fixed parities if growth is pursued. (The real mystery of the French expansion in 1983 is how they thought they thought they could have expansion and 'franc fort'.)

But while the French failure looms large in the we-are-powerless Labour modernising mind, the experience of Britain leaving the ERM in 1992, does not. Yet what happened in 1992 when Britain was forced out of the ERM in 1992 by these 'global forces' we are supposed to fear so much? Dire consequences were predicted if the pound left the ERM, notably a massive increase in inflation. (Being in the ERM was claimed to be a guaranteed anti-inflation measure by both Labour and Conservative economics spokespersons.) The world's currency dealers concluded that, at D-mark 2.95, the pound was seriously overvalued – a view shared by a wide section of British economists and, we are led to believe, despite their silence on the subject at the time, the Labour Shadow Cabinet.[39] The Conservative Government tried to defend an unrealistic exchange rate by the usual means – giving the Bank of England's reserves away to speculators – and then recognised defeat. The value of sterling fell, and none of the predictions of economic disaster turned out to be true. Inflation did not shoot up; domestic production expanded with the more competitive pound, exports expanded and unemployment fell. In direct refutation of everything Labour's economics spokespersons apparently believed, the relatively good economic position inherited by the Blair government in 1997 is a direct consequence of the British economy leaving the ERM.

In the *Independent on Sunday* of 15 January 1996, Alastair Darling, now Treasury Minister, was quoted as saying, 'It is not up to the government to say that the banks can only make so much profit.' It certainly used to be 'up to the government': even Geoffrey Howe imposed a windfall tax on the banks in 1981; but that was back in those far-off days before the Government handed power to set interest rates, perhaps the most powerful single economic tool and the surest means of regulating how much banks earn, to the people who stand to gain by putting them up! Just before the 1997 General Election Roy Hattersley wrote in his *Guardian* column of meeting one of the then Labour shadow economics team, who told him that in the new global economy it was not possible for a government to increase taxes.[40]

On his visit to the beleaguered Bill Clinton in February 1998, Tony Blair told Guardian journalist and long-time Blair ally, Martin Kettle, of the 'five clear principles of the centre-left'. The first of these was: '. . . stable management and economic prudence because of the global economy.'[41]

The acid test for Labour 'modernisers' has become how completely you accept the powerlessness thesis. The line sounds immediately plausible to those, like New Labour economics spokespersons, with little economic knowledge: it is what they keep reading in the newspapers and being told by their advisers from the City. The powerlessness thesis also has the advantage of being a popular line with Labour supporters of the European Union who can argue, as the Labour Party has done since it became Euro-enthusiasts, that we need Europe to control capital ('the speculators'). A decade ago Gordon Brown *et al* believed that British membership of the ERM would do it; when that failed they concluded that only a single currency would do it. But the propositions that nation states are powerless against capital movements, or that the free market model is the only one possible (or successful) are immediately falsified by the experience of Norway, and the Asian variants of corporatist, producer alliance, restrictive, trade barrier and exchange control-laden, nationalist economies of the Far East. These so-called 'tiger' economies had developed and grown in defiance of Anglo-American free market theories[42]

Why have New Labour adopted the powerlessness thesis? In part, it is simply that they are in the grip of theories; and like most people in the grip of theories they exclude information which might challenge them. The theories are reinforced by the fact that they are those currently approved of by their mentors in the United States and the British overseas lobby. In so far as alternative views are perceived, they are offered by people who for one reason or another, are regarded by New Labour as either discredited, such as the Labour Left, or beyond the pale, such as the Tory Europhobes. Thirdly, and most importantly, New Labour politicians like the belief that they are powerless against the world's financial markets. Powerless as they are, a range of things that Labour leaders used to have try to deliver – growth, economic justice, redistribution – have ceased to be rational expectations of them. Nothing can be done short of the European-wide level; and maybe not even then.[43] Life is infinitely easier for Labour economic ministers when all they have to do is follow the City's line.

Notes

1   Martin Kettle, *The Guardian* 3 February 1996

2   *The Observer* 14 April 1996. This visit is missing from John Rentoul's biography of Blair, *Tony Blair*, (London: Little Brown, 1995).

3   Gordon Brown, with the late John Smith, attended the 1991 meeting at Baden-Baden. (This is not included in his 1998 biography by Paul Routledge.) The full list of those attending was published in the US magazine *The Spotlight* 22 July 1991. This article with others from the same source on the Bilderberg group and Trilateral Commission can be found on the net at <www.real.net.au/insurge/ politics/global_power/nword.htm/> *The Spotlight* is undoubtedly a racist magazine. Nonetheless it is the only magazine which consistently prints articles about trans-national forums like Bilderberg and Trilateral. Monks attended the meeting in 1996. The list of those attending the 1996 meeting was published in Canada and then put up on the net. Tony Blair's Bilderberg meeting is in his Parliamentary declaration of interests.

4   *The Guardian* 3 October 1994.

5   Ken Coates and Michael Barrett Brown suggest in their book *The Blair Revelation* (Nottingham: Spokesman, 1996) that Powell's job in the British embassy in Washington concealed a role as the liaison officer between British intelligence and the CIA, but they have no evidence. Powell's career summary as given in *The Diplomatic Service List* for 1995 contains nothing from which to directly infer an intelligence role. He was born in 1956 and joined the FCO (Foreign and Commonwealth Office) in 1979. Since then he was Third later Second Secretary in Lisbon, 1981; Second later First Secretary at the FCO, London; UK delegate to CDE Stockholm 1986; UK delegate at the CSCE in Vienna 1986; First Secretary FCO, London 1989; then First Secretary (Chancery) Washington 1991.

6   *The Guardian* 3 October 1994. Balls was profiled in *The Guardian* (G2) 16 March 1998.

7   *The Sunday Telegraph* 24 March 1996. Davies was an adviser to the Callaghan

Government as a member of the Downing Street Policy Unit, headed by (now Sir) Bernard Donoghue. He was included in the party which visited President Clinton in early 1998.

8 *Who's Who* 1992.

9 Peter Hennessy, 'The View from Here', in *The Independent* (Education) 1 May 1997.

10 Mandelson 'flunked first year exams because he was spending all his time working as president of the United Nations Association's youth and student branch.' The Independent 1 July 1989.

11 On WAY see the scattering of references in Joel Kotek's *Students and the Cold War*, (London: Macmillan,1996), Joseph B. Smith, *Portrait of a Cold Warrior*, (New York: Ballantine, 1981) and Jonathan Bloch and Patrick Fitzgerald, *British Intelligence and Covert Action*, (London: Junction, 1983).

12 *The Independent* 29 July 1995. McIntyre is reported (1998) to be writing a biography of Mandelson.

13 See Tom Easton's 'The British American Project for the Successor Generation', in *Lobster* 33.

14 On which see, for example 'The AFL-CIA' in Howard Frazier (ed.) *Uncloaking the CIA* (New York: The Free Press, 1978) and Peter E. Newell, 'The International Centre of Free Trade Unionists in Exile' in *Lobster* 31.

15 These paragraphs on TUCETU are taken from David Osler's 'American and Tory Intervention in the British Unions since the 1970s' in *Lobster* 33.

16 *The Times* 17 July 1995.

17 The non-EU section of overseas UK capital, located chiefly in the US, the Commonwealth and the Republic of South Africa, is less enthusiastic about EU membership. Their views are expressed most clearly in *The Sunday Telegraph*.

18 An unnamed 'businessman close to the Labour leadership' said in *The Observer* (Business)13 April 1997, p. 5: 'The big companies – the ones who do the most trading with Europe – are really worried about the xenophobe right.'

19 See his review of *Defeat from the Jaws of Victory: Inside Kinnock's Labour Party* by Heffernan and Maquesee, in *The Guardian* 15 December 1992.

20 Cited in Eric Shaw's 'The Evolution of Labour's Campaign Strategy 1987-91: some Preliminary Notes and Comments', a paper presented at the Conference of the Political Studies Association, Queen's University, Belfast 7-9 April 1992. Thanks to John Booth for this.

21 Faber and Faber, 1996, p. 12.

22 Frank Blackaby, 'Exchange Rate Policy and Economic Strategy' in *Three Banks Review*, June 1980.

23 Nicholas Ridley, *My Style of Government*, (London: Hutchinson, 1991), p. 71.

24 Cecil Parkinson, *Right at the Centre*, (London: Weidenfeld and Nicolson, 1992) pp. 238 and 9.

25 In the 1000 plus pages of Nigel Lawson's memoir, there are only four indexed references to the manufacturing sector, in the last of which he comments that if North Sea oil has 'crowded out' manufacturing, then as North Sea oil declines, it

will spontaneously 'crowd back in'. See his *The View from No. 11* (London: Corgi, 1992) p. 196.

26 *The Guardian 8* January 1992.

27 The 'Treasury knights' are the Permanent Secretaries. I asked Pearce who he was quoting but while he did not identify the Treasury official, he commented: 'I'm pretty sure that factory-despising attitudes are common in the Treasury though not universal.' Letter to author 14 January 1992.

28 See Nick Cohen's 'Why is CIA ex-agent setting our interest rates?' in *The Observer* 19 October 1997. Ms Julius, now with British Airways, worked as an analyst for the CIA.

29 *The Independent* 12 May 1997.

30 7 February 1998.

31 See for example Neil Kinnock's *Making Our Way* (Blackwell, 1986).

32 *The Guardian* 7 July 1997.

33 *The Guardian* 11 July 1997.

34 *The Guardian* 5 December 1997.

35 *The Guardian* 18 February 1998. She repeated this central 'line' in an exchange of letters with Austin Mitchell MP. See Larry Elliot, *The Guardian* 9 March 1998.

36 See, for example, the leader 'Manufacturing a recession' in *The Guardian* 20 January 1998.

37 See, for example, the arguments by Labour economics adviser Gavyn Davies, in *The Independent* 12 May 1997, and the replies in the Letters on 14 May.

38 On this see Seamus Milne, 'A French lesson for the left' in *Tribune* 26 March 1993.

39 Neil Kinnock's assistant at the time, Neil Stewart, commented that the reason Kinnock did not express his belief that pound was overvalued was, 'It's a dickhead says it before the Tories.' *Rintoul* p. 267.

40 Hattersley declined to tell me the name of this person. My guess? Alastair Darling. This was an echo of Tony Blair's 1996 comment in Japan that, 'We also recognise that in a global economy . . . our tax rates need to be internationally as well as nationally competitive.' Blair p. 123.

41 *The Guardian* 7 February 1998.

42 This was written just before the 1998 collapse of the so-called Asian 'tiger' economies. As far as I can see the collapse is chiefly the result of those economies reducing the restrictions which used to exist, in pursuit of the western free market model, thus encouraging speculation (aka 'investment') by their domestic and Euro-American financial sectors – with the usual disastrous results. On Norway see Larry Elliot in *The Guardian* 6 April 1998.

43 General Secretary of the TUC, John Monks, called in 1996 for 'world works councils for each major international company', *The Guardian* 31 January 1996. International capitalism did not noticeably tremble at this absurd prospect. Against the globalisation-nation-state-is-powerless thesis, see for example Martin Wolf 'Far From Powerless' in *The Financial Times* 13 May 1997; 'Grand National idea produces winners', Larry Elliot, *The Guardian* 20 October 1997, 'Don't be fooled: multinationals do not rule the world', *Independent on Sunday* 12 January 1997 and 'Globaloney', Paul Hirst in *Prospect* February 1996.

BIBLIOGRAPHY

Bain, Donald. *The Control of Candy Jones* (London: Futura, 1976)

Bamford, James. *Body of Secrets* (New York: Anchor, 2002)

Bergier, Jacques and Pauwels, Louis. *The Dawn of Magic* (London: Panther, 1964)

Bloch, Jonathan and Fitzgerald, Patrick. *British Intelligence and Covert Action* (London: Junction, 1983)

Bowart, Walter. *Operation Mind Control* (London: Fontana, 1978)

Brook-Shepherd, Gordon. *The Storm Birds* (London: Weidenfeld and Nicolson, 1988)

Caro, Robert A. *The Years of Lyndon Johnson: Master of the Senate* (New York: Alfred A. Knopf, 2002)

Dorril, Stephen. *MI6* (London: Fourth Estate, 2000)

Freeman, Simon, with Penrose, Barrie. *Rinkagate* (London: Bloomsbury, 1997)

Freedman, Lawrence. *US Intelligence and the Soviet Strategic Theatre* (London: Macmillan, 1986)

Hepburn, James. (pseudonym) *Farewell America* (Vaduz [Lichenstein]: Frontiers, 1968)

Kinnock, Neil. *Making Our Way* (Oxford: Blackwell, 1987)

Kitson, Frank. *Low Intensity Operations* (London: Faber and Faber, 1971)

Gordiefsky, Oleg and Andrew, Christopher. *KGB: The Inside Story* (London: Hodder and Stoughton, 1990)

Lifton, David. *Best Evidence* (New York: Carroll and Graf, 1980)

Manham, Patrick. *Trail of Destruction* (London: Viking, 1987)

Marks, John. *The Search for the 'Manchurian Candidate'* (London: Allan Lane, 1979)

Michell, John. *The Flying Saucer Vision* (London: Abacus, 1974)

Ostrander, Sheila and Schroder, Lynn. *Psychic Discoveries Behind the Iron Curtain* (London: Bantam, 1971)

Penrose, Barry and Courtiour, Roger. *The Pencourt File* (London: Secker and Warburg, 1978)

Porter, Bernard. *The Origins of the Vigilant State* (London: Weidenfeld and Nicolson, 1987)

Quigley, Carroll. *Tragedy and Hope* (New York: Macmillan, 1966)

Rintoul, John. *Tony Blair* (London: Little brown, 1995)

Sklar, Holly. (ed.) *Trilateralism* (Boston: South End Press, 1980)

Suvorov, Victor. (pseudonym) *The Liberators* (London: Hamish Hamilton, 1981)

Thayer, George. *The British Political Fringe* (London: Anthony Blond, 1965)

Winter, Gordon. *Inside BOSS* (London: Penguin, 1981)

Wright, Peter. *Spycatcher* (New York: Viking, 1987)

INDEX